# Prayers That Break Curses and Spells and Release Favors and Breakthroughs

*Powerful Prayers & Declarations for Breaking Curses and Spells and Commanding Favors in Your Life*

### Daniel C. Okpara

Copyright © July 2016 by Daniel C. Okpara.

All Rights Reserved. Do not reproduce contents of this book in any way or by any means without written consent of the publisher, except brief excerpts in critical reviews and articles.

---

Published By:

**Better Life Media.**

BETTER LIFE WORLD OUTREACH CENTER.

Website: www.BetterLifeWorld.org

Email: info@betterlifeworld.org

---

### FOLLOW US ON FACEBOOK

1. **Like our Page on Facebook** for updates

2. **Join Our Facebook Prayer Group**, submit prayer requests and follow powerful daily prayers for total victory and breakthrough

---

This book title and others are obtainable for quantity discounts for sale promotions, gifts, and evangelism. Visit our website or email us to get started.

---

All scripture quotation in this book is culled from the New King James Version or New International Version, except where stated. Used by permission.

# Table of Contents

FREE BONUS  iv

RECEIVE DAILY AND WEEKLY PRAYERS  v

Acknowledgments  6

Introduction  7

Chapter 1: What is a Curse And A Spell?  11

Chapter 2: Types Of Curses  20

Chapter 3: Signs Of Curses And Spells  57

Chapter 4: Getting Rid of Curses and Spells  62

Chapter 5: Prayers to Destroy Curses and Spells  83

Chapter 6:  How to Maintain Your Deliverance  142

Get in Touch  148

About the Author  149

Other Books By the Same Author  151

NOTES  154

# FREE BONUS

Download These 4 Powerful Books Today for FREE... And Take Your Relationship With God to a New Level.

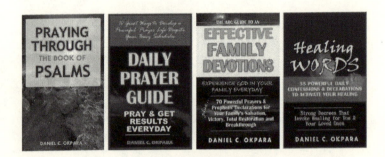

**Download below**

www.betterlifeworld.org/grow

# RECEIVE DAILY AND WEEKLY PRAYERS

**Powerful Prayers Sent to Your Inbox Every Monday**

Enter your email address to receive notifications of new posts, prayers and prophetic declarations sent to you by email.

[Email Address]

[Sign Me Up]

*Go to: **BreakThroughPrayers.org** to subscribe to receive FREE WEEKLY PRAYER POINTS, and prophetic declarations sent to you by email.*

# Acknowledgments

Isaac, Annabel and Excel are three great children who'll teach you how to pay attention. I've had to learn beginner academic classes, so I don't fail their questions. I'm grateful to God for choosing me to father these gifts. May they grow in God's strength and wisdom.

Thanks to my friends, partners and all ministry staff who stand by me every day, and encourage me to continue to thrive. May God bless you all.

# Introduction

*"I call heaven and earth as witnesses today against you, that I have set before you life and death, blessing and cursing; therefore choose life, that both you and your descendants may live"* – **Deut. 30:19.**

Life is comprised of two equal and opposite extremes: They are up and down, good and evil, God and Satan, blessings and curses. While blessings produce good results, such as life, peace, good health, and progress, curses produce evil ends, such as shame, frustration, pain, sickness, fear, failure and death.

According to the Scripture, we have the power to choose which divide we want. Yes, you can choose to be cursed or be blessed.

However, God counsels us to choose blessing and reject curse. He advises us to accept life so that our children and we may live.

This book is designed to empower you to pray for yourself and obtain deliverance from curses, spells, and other unknown problems you may be going through at the moment.

Instead of running around looking for some man of God to pray for you, you'll be motivated to:

***"Deliver yourself as a roe from the hand of the hunter, and as a bird from the hand of the fowler*** (Proverbs 6:5).

Yes, I want to drag you through the "painful" but rewarding journey of delivering yourself - moving from victim to victor, from pain to gain, from weeping to celebration, from sickness to perfect health, and from curse to blessing.

I want to provoke you to be your own greatest prophet and change your life with God's power in the next 30-90 days.

In this book, you'll learn the secret behind strange problems, unexplainable health situations, severe financial difficulties, persistent nightmares, sudden losses, and inexplicable hatred. You'll see behind the veil why there are mysterious circumstances that are beyond human explanations. You'll understand why the subject of curses must be well understood and mastered by any person who truly wants to live a victorious life in Christ.

Once you learn the lessons in this book, you'll be dangerously equipped to become your own prophet. You'll be able to hear the voice of God for yourself and bring these attacks on your health, finances, relationship, and family to their knees.

You'll rise and say no to:

- Job losses and career frustrations
- Infertility and other reproductive failures
- Shame and disgrace
- Attacks on your health
- Attacks on your finances

- Attacks on your marriage and relationships

- Attacks on your dreams

- The stranglehold of debts, etc

You'll take what belongs to you in Christ and live a victorious life.

Amen.

# Chapter 1: What is a Curse And A Spell?

Several years ago, a man went to a family to seek the hand of a 10-year old girl in marriage. The father was amazed, took it as a joke, and told the man that his daughter was only a kid. However, the man gushed on and on how he truly loved the girl and would want her to be his wife. But when he saw he wasn't making sense, he left and promised to be back when the girl had grown up. True to his words, three years later, he went back to seek the hand of the same girl, now 13, in marriage. *"She's grown now,"* he said.

The girl's father became annoyed. And after a back and forth argument, he sternly warned the suitor to stay away from his family. He yelled for the umpteenth time that his daughters would go to the University before thinking about marriage.

Unfortunately, the strange man felt offended and betrayed, and pronounced curses over the man and his children (the girls) and left.

No one took him seriously. They saw his curses as an expression of his annoyance and frustration. So they didn't bother. Life moved on.

But many years later, the girls from the family would finish school and would not be married. It became a thing of concern when they were crossing age forty, and no proposals were coming. Eventually, one, out of the four daughters started looking for answers. After several prayers, going from place to place, doing lots of in-searching, the father told them what happened when they were still kids. Although he didn't think that had anything to do with their situation.

But to the glory of God, the family came together, prayed and renounced curses and claimed deliverance in Jesus Christ. The curse was reversed and broken, and the ladies started getting married.

## UNDERSTANDING WHAT A CURSE AND A SPELL IS

Curses and spells have the power to impose invisible barriers in someone's life. They can affect someone's health, business, and relationship in a very negative way.

The Cambridge Dictionary has the following definitions for the word, **curse**:

- To use a word or an expression that is not polite and shows that you are outraged.

- To say magic words that are intended to bring bad luck to someone.

- Magic words that are intended to bring bad luck to someone.

- A cause of trouble and unhappiness.

- A rude word or phrase

- To say rude or offensive words about something or someone because you are angry

- To wish for something evil or unpleasant to happen to someone or something, as by asking a magical power.

- Something evil or unpleasant that happens to someone or something, by or as if by magical power.

A *spell,* on the other hand, is a form of words used as a supernatural appeal or invocation to control or influence someone or something. Other words for spell include incantation, charm, conjuration, sorcery, magic, witchcraft, witchery, hex, mojo, *makutua*, etc.

From these definitions, we see that **curse or cursing** is more than using foul language, profane words, or perhaps, even blasphemous words when one is angry. Our classification of a **curse** as swearwords used to express displeasure or anger is but only a small portion of what *curse*, *cursing*, or *curses* mean. When these swearwords have certain characteristics, they are no longer anger expressions, but dangerous curses.

I define curse as a reason for suffering. It is the application of spiritual law that allows or brings judgments and their penalties upon a person or a people.

A curse or spell can be a reason for adverse events in someone's life. It can be responsible for the harm and pain that someone is going through. Sickness, calamity, or other unfortunate situations can be a product of a curse in operation.

---

*When swearwords are used as incantations, evil projections, or spiritual arrows, with an intense wish for evil - before witchdoctors, shamans, mediums, soothsayers, seers, fortunetellers, elders, and magicians - they become compelling tools of torment. They become curses because they are no longer in the category of normal vibration of an angry person.*

---

When those who have authority over others speak swearwords, the words become dangerous and produce the effects of curses on the victims. For example, parents' curses on their children will produce the effects of curses; teachers' curses on their wards will produce the effects of curses; a husband's constant curse on his wife will produce the effect of evils, and so on.

People also attract curses when they break universal laws that have in-built consequences. For instance, incest, murder, abortion, all forms of sexual perversion, adultery, abusing and hurting parents, and others, will invoke curses because these sins break universal laws.

You will also invoke curses into operation if you continually and habitually speak negative words about yourself. This is because you have authority over your life. That is why the Bible says that death and life are in the power of the tongue.

Curses are also triggered when binding agreements are broken without minding the obvious consequences issued when the deal was made. For example, if two young people, out of lustful love, drink their blood promising to marry themselves or else this and that will happen. If one party breaks this agreement, they will undoubtedly trigger the effects of curses. The same thing applies in other forms of contracts and covenants.

## What The Bible Says About Curses

In the King James Version of The Bible, the word **curse** is mentioned 101 times. While the word **curses** and **cursed**, together, appear over 80 times.

According to Strong's Concordance, the word curse (and cursing) mostly used in the Bible is from the Greek word, **Katara**, pronounced *kat-ar'-ah*. It means what has to go down; that is, what has to happen as a penalty for something.

In simple terms, the Bible doesn't see curse or curses as an ordinary expression of anger using bad words. It sees it as:

- Punishment for something done, and or
- Words that have the power to cause harm

The book of Deuteronomy 30:19 says: *I call heaven and earth as witnesses today against you, that I have set before you life and death,* ***blessing and cursing****; therefore choose life, that both you and your descendants may live.*

As blessing produce life – health, peace, opportunities, progress - curse produce death – hardship, sickness, lack of progress, confusion, quarrel, and other sufferings.

The Bible is filled with examples of *curses* and *cursings*. Here are a few:

- God cursed the serpent for enticing Adam and Eve (Genesis. 3:13-15)

- The ground was cursed for Adam and Eve's sake (Genesis. 3:17-19).

- Cain was cursed for killing Abel (Genesis. 4:11–16)

- Noah cursed his grandson, Canaan, and his descendants for his father's disrespect (Gen. 9:25–27)

- Israel will be blessed if they obey God, and cursed if they disobey (Deut. 28, and Deut. 29:18–28).

- Elisha cursed his servant, Gehazi and his descendants, for lying in the name of God. They would be afflicted with leprosy as a result of this curse (2 Kings. 5:20-27).

- Jesus cursed the unproductive fig tree, and it died (Mark 11:11-14, 20–21).

- Cities that rejected the Gospel were cursed (Luke 10:10-15).

- Rebelling against God's established laws brings terrible curses (Deut. 11:26-28, 28:15-60).

God said to Abraham: *"And I will bless them that bless thee, and curse him that curseth thee: and in thee shall all families of the earth be blessed."*

He was simply telling Abraham: *"Some people will try to curse you – they will try to use their words to harm you, to try to stop my plans for you – but don't worry, I'll be your insurance against them."*

**If a person is under a curse, according to the Bible, evil has come upon them in some way.**

The world that Abraham lived in is the same world that we also live in. We still have men and women willing to be tools of evil, trying to use curses (sorcery, witchcraft, voodoo, black magic, and other ways) to bring sufferings on others. There are also curses we bring on ourselves through negative words, breaking universal laws, breaking covenants and agreements, disobeying divine instructions, inheritance, and so on. Let us examine how these curses work, and seek deliverance from them through the name and Blood of Jesus Christ.

## Chapter 2: Types Of Curses

*₁₃Is anyone among you suffering? Let him pray. Is anyone cheerful? Let him sing psalms. ₁₄Is anyone among you sick? Let him call for the elders of the church, and let them pray over him, anointing him with oil in the name of the Lord. ₁₅And the prayer of faith will save the sick, and the Lord will raise him up. And if he has committed sins, he will be forgiven.*

*₁₆Confess your trespasses to one another, and pray for one another, that you may be healed. The effective, fervent prayer of a righteous man avails much. -* **James 5:13-16**

There are two significant levels of healing James is talking about here. First, when one is sick, they can call for or request prayers. As they are anointed with oil and are prayed for, they'll be forgiven and healed. But there's another level he talks about. In verse 16 he says to confess your trespasses to one another so that you can also be healed. This is another level of healing and deliverance when the situation is not just a normal sickness that anointing with oil takes care of.

In our ministry to others, we've encountered many situations that anointing with oil didn't resolve, until the persons spoke up, revealed some things they knew about or had done; then together, we present the situations to the Lord seeking His mercy. And then the healing and deliverance take place.

The most important thing to note in seeking deliverance from curses is to be willing to open up. Be willing to speak up. Don't try to hide your sins and say I've confessed them to the Lord. Or try to protect any information you know may help with prayers, thinking, *"Well, let the Lord show him the issue if he's a man/woman of God."*

That's a wrong way to think. You don't go to your doctor and say, *"well, Doctor, you have to figure out my problem before I'll know you're a qualified doctor."* No. You speak up, and together you both can find a solution to the problem.

That is the same thing you need to do when seeking spiritual help. If you seek prayer from someone, according to James, you'll need to open up. And if you don't trust your privacy safe with the person, then don't go requesting prayer from the person in the first place.

Here are a few types of curses I have learned from our ministry to others. Sometimes people may have more than one of these curses working in their lives. But the good news is that all curses can be nullified in Jesus name.

## 1. Self-Imposed Curses

The words you speak to yourself every day, about your life, career, future and home are working for or against you in many ways, because you have divine authority over your life. If you regularly speak faith-filled words, you create blessings as returns. But if you continuously speak fear-filled words, you create curses in return.

The book of Proverbs 18:21 says: *"Death and life are in the power of the tongue, and those who love it will eat its fruit."*

Jesus said, *"For by your words you will be justified, and by your words, you will be condemned"* (Matthew 12:37).

Self-imposed curses are curses that you have placed over yourself by the use of negative confessions and responses. For example, if I ask you and say, *'how's life?'*

And you say…

- *'Men, it's not easy.'*

- *'Things are so hard now.'*

- *'I've tried all I could, but there is no way.'*

- *'I'm just parching and managing.'*

- *'I'm dying.'*

- *'There is no hope.'*

- *'These children will kill me.'*

- *'This job is killing me.'*

- *'I'm just wasting away here.'*

- *'My husband is just a big pain in the ass.'*

- *'My wife is troublesome. She is killing me.'*

- *'This economy is biting so hard.'*

- *'I just keep getting frustrated and frustrated.'*

- *'I'll be dead soon.'*

- *'This child is just so hopeless.'*

Using words like these may seem that you're just stating how things are at the moment, but those are strong negative affirmations that eventually create those realities. The Bible says:

**Proverbs 13:3** - *He who guards his mouth preserves his life, but he who opens wide his lips shall have destruction.*

**Proverbs 16:24** - *Pleasant words are like a honeycomb, sweetness to the soul and health to the bones.*

**Proverbs 21:23** - *Whoever guards his mouth and tongue keeps his soul from troubles.*

Matthew 15:18 - *But those things which proceed out of the mouth come from the heart, and they defile a man.*

Ephesians 4:29 - *Let no corrupt word proceed out of your mouth, but what is good for necessary edification, that it may impart grace to the hearers.*

The scriptures are not joking with these warnings. Your words can make or mar you. As we learn to revoke all kinds of curses, it's essential to accept God's correction and instruction for avoiding these curses entirely.

Fifteen years or so ago, we had this friend of ours who was very prayerful. We always envied his prayer life. He would wake up in the midnight and pray for four hours or more at a stretch. Usually, when you wake up to pray, he's praying. When you're done praying, he's still praying. No one could match his prayer life.

Unfortunately, ask him about life, and you'll hear the worse negative words from him. When he speaks, he speaks of discouragement, fear, failure, and how life has messed him up. We usually wonder how he's able to spend hours praying and never sees anything positive about life. Try to encourage him, and he'll tell you to forget about it. It was a paradox too profound for us to comprehend.

Yes, he had experienced a lot of challenges before discerning the call of God for his life. Sadly, these setbacks had eaten too deep into him that irrespective of his powerful prayer life, he didn't expect much from life, and he was always quick to admit it in conversations. Guess what: a few years ago, that's like thirteen years after, when I bumped into him, his experiences hadn't changed much from the things he always spoke about many years ago.

---

*The truth is that life is not easy; we all experience challenges and setbacks day in day out. But the best we can do to ourselves is being positive.*

---

We must not allow our problems to define our words and expectations for the future. If we do, these words can become self-imposed curses against us, working and creating more limitations that we'll always wonder where our problems are coming from.

## 2. The Curse of Parents

Have you ever wondered why the first commandment with a promise attached to it has to do with our relationship with our parents? The Book of Ephesians 6:1-3 says, *"Children, obey your parents in the Lord, for this is right. 'Honor your father and mother,' which is the first commandment with promise: 'that it may be well with you and you may live long on the earth.'"*

Except God's love for us, a parent's love is the strongest and most enduring love that exists in the world. Yes, our parents may not always be right, but dishonoring and causing them pain creates problems for us eventually.

> *Whoever curses his father or his mother, his lamp will be put out in deep darkness (Proverbs 20:20).*

The Amplified Bible renders this verse thus: *'Whoever curses his father or his mother, his lamp of life will be extinguished in time of darkness.'* While the Living Bible says, *'God puts out the light of the man who curses his father or mother.'*

Dishonoring your parents, hurting them, or mistreating them, puts you in enmity with God. That is, God will be the one fighting you. Yes, you'll fast, pray, have hands laid on you, yet the problem doesn't get solved, because God is the one responsible for what you're going through – as a result of treating your parents unfairly.

This is one of the biggest mysteries I've seen working against many people, including Christians. You can't treat your parents like they're nothing and expect life to be fair to you.

I was praying with a lady some time ago and was inspired to tell her to call her mother and ask for her prayers and blessings. She later said to me, *"When I called my mom and told her I was calling to ask her forgiveness and blessings, she was stunned. After all said and done, she told me I have done the right thing, and therefore it would be well with me."*

"But pastor," she continued. *"I never expected that my mom had some unsaid grievances against me. I thought all was well all these years."*

Sometimes we have maltreated our parents, and out of love, they kept it all inside themselves. They never spoke out. Unfortunately, these actions of disrespect trigger spiritual curses to operate.

The Bible says:

**Cursed is anyone who dishonors their father or mother. Then all the people shall say, "Amen!"** - Deuteronomy 27:16

**The eye that mocks a father and scorns to obey a mother will be picked out by the ravens of the valley and eaten by the vultures.** - Proverbs 30:17

If you've disrespected your parents in the past, go back and say sorry. By going back to say sorry and getting their blessings, you'll stop many unknown sufferings in your life.

Dr. B.C Ebere is a man of God I highly admire. He has been in the ministry for close to forty years and always does his best to encourage upcoming ministers on the power and benefits of integrity and patience while pursuing God's call for their lives. Some time ago, he shared a story that made an enormous impact on my life.

One day he got worried that he was not experiencing results commensurate with his efforts and prayers in the ministry. So he decided to fast and pray and ask for divine direction. While praying, the LORD revealed to him that he had disrespected his father many years ago and needed to get his father's blessing.

That was a startling revelation because he had been in ministry for close to 20 years then. And as far as he could tell, he did not have any grudges with his dad. He thought his dad was okay with him.

Well, the Bible says that obedience is better than sacrifice, so he decided to obey. He bought gifts and took them to his old man and pleaded with him to forgive if there was any way he had disrespected him in the time past. Surprisingly, the old man still remembered an incidence of disrespect and letdown he had caused him while growing up as a young man. He hadn't forgotten that event, even though it was many years ago. They discussed it, and he prayed for him.

He spent some time with his dad and then returned to his ministry base. Two weeks later, someone gave him a car gift. A month or so later, another person gave him a plot of land. He started getting so blessed that he wondered why he didn't discover this and do this earlier.

You see, the truth is that our parents may not have been so kind to us. But they are still the source we came into this world. We must do the best we can to honor them and get their blessings. The simple act of getting our parent's blessings has the power to neutralize many years of hardship.

Don't forget that your parents here also connote your foster parents, guardians, and those who took care of you as a child. Getting their blessings and forgiveness can have profound positive impact on your life.

I know there are exceptions, like when we have been abused and treated like shits by our parents. However, even in such situations, we must not ascribe judgment and vengeance to ourselves. We must forgive, pray for them, and seek their blessings, not because we have not been hurt, but because we must move forward. The person who forgives actually does himself a greater good.

As parents also, the words that we speak to and over our children have strong powers to create their realities eventually. Let us, therefore, watch with care how we release words over our kids, even when we are provoked and trying to caution them. There's got to be a balance in it all as the scriptures say in Colossians 3:20-21:

> $_{20}$*Children, obey your parents in everything. This pleases the Lord. $_{21}$Fathers, don't upset your children. If you are too hard to please, they might want to stop trying* (ERV).

## 3. The Curse Of Spiritual Disobedience

Neglecting spiritual signals, God's leading, and divine direction also produce the effects of curses. As the Bible says, *"To obey is better than sacrifice, and to heed is better than the fat of rams. For rebellion is as serious as the sin of divination (fortune-telling and witchcraft), and disobedience is as serious as false religion and idolatry. Because you have rejected the word of the Lord, He also has rejected you..." (1 Sam. 15:22-24 - AMP)*

When we fail to recognize and follow God's leading in our hearts, it is capable of closing our heavens. We may spend years praying and fasting without commensurate answers. We may give fat offerings and make substantial financial sacrifices to support the poor and the church, yet not experience God's answers to our prayers, because we are not in His will for our lives.

Our utmost desire as children of God should be to be able to recognize how and when God is speaking to our hearts about something and yield in obedience. Obedience is the key to God's blessings and protection.

Let me tell you a story.

In July 2009, I registered a company, and in 2010, I went into a business partnership with two of my friends. Our business was around forex trading and investment in the stock markets. Having traded the markets for over four years and worked with several brokers in real time before then, I seemed to have a lot of experience on my shelf. Combined with the skills of two of my partners in the banking industry and stock market, we looked very qualified to run a profitable company.

We decided to raise funds for trading, and it wasn't long before people started investing with us. Our terms were that their capitals were secured, no matter what. Things were looking so good that one could look at tomorrow and believe that we were made.

But there was a small problem. Inside me, the CEO of the company, I had this uncomfortable feeling that all was not going to be well. I was just uneasy about the whole arrangement - the partnership, the business, everything. I couldn't see any physical reason for this ***"uncomfortability,"*** because all seemed to be in order. The money was coming in, people were responding to our business plan, we had spent days praying, fasting, and sowing seeds in different ministries for divine backing, so why the inner fear? Why the internal discomfort?

I called my friends and told them that we need to dissolve this business and refund our investors right away. I didn't have any other proof except that I know that this inner discomfort was a sign of danger ahead. It was a sign of God's leading. Unfortunately, the accountant used figures to prove me wrong. So we had to continue.

Fast forward. In 2011, we made some wrong investments and lost every fund with us. We wound up and ran into massive debts, followed with all manner of crisis. The investors, all of them, wanted their monies back. And so began a long fight that has lasted several years, a fight that only the grace of God is helping to see us through.

---

*You see, God knows the end before the beginning. In most cases, He will try to direct us, but being creatures of choices, He leaves the responsibility with us.*

---

Sometimes, we know precisely inside of us what to do regarding a situation, but ignore it and move on. In our spirits, we have this feeling that **'this is wrong and this is how to proceed.'** But we would often prefer to pray for more visible signs and confirmations. We may be expecting some sky shakings, loud voices, and dreams. But God does not work that way.

I believe that spiritual disobedience attracts the biggest of all curses in life. We invite this curse when we willfully disobey the inner witness of the Holy Spirit in us or other forms of divine direction. The Bible says:

*He opens their ear to instruction, and commands that they return from evil. If they hear and serve Him, they will end their days in prosperity and their years in pleasures. But if they do not listen, they shall perish by the sword, and they will die without knowledge –*
Job 36: 10-12

Look at that scripture. The Bible is saying that if we do not pay attention to God's leading and instructions in our hearts, we'll perish by the sword, and die without knowledge. This is not talking about eternal damnation, but exposure to sufferings and evil situations that can get us to the point of death.

Are there things the Lord is laying in your heart, and you know it? Can you look back and recollect so many ways that the Lord has tried to guide and instruct your heart that you ignored? This type of disobedience has the power to invoke the effects of curses in operation against your life. Go to God in humility, repent and seek His mercy.

The Bible says:

*₂₂Which pleases the Lord more: burnt offerings and sacrifices or obeying his commands? It is better to obey the Lord than to offer sacrifices to him. It is better to listen to him than to offer the fat from rams.*

*₂₃**Refusing to obey is as bad as the sin of witchcraft. Being stubborn and doing what you want is like the sin of worshiping idols**. You refused to obey the Lord's command, so he now refuses to accept you as king"* (1 Samuel 15:22-23 - ERV).

## 4. Inherited Curses

You and I came from God. But you also notice that God did not throw us down from the sky to live on this earth. We passed through a means – a parent.

There is a gate to this world. And that gate is being born through a woman by the empowering of a man. Anyone who doesn't pass through that gate is an illegal person. God could have thrown Jesus down from the sky to live with us. But he didn't do that. Why? Because no one would accept him and his mission.

Ever wonder why Jesus said: *"₁Most assuredly, I say to you, he who does not enter the sheepfold by the door, but climbs up some other way, the same is a thief and a robber. ₂But he who comes by the door is the shepherd of the sheep. ₃To him, the doorkeeper opens, and the sheep hear his voice, and he calls his own sheep by name and leads them out.* - John 10:1-3.

He is simply telling us that he came to this world through the *"gate,"* for we know he is the Shepherd and Bishop of our souls. And that we should identify anyone who comes by other means as a thief and a robber. In verse 10 he stated it clearly – Satan! Yes, Satan and all his demons are thieves and robbers. They do not have right into this world because they didn't come through the gate. You have more right in this world than satan and his demons – because you came through the right gate into the world - and you can stand on that right and claim your blessings and spiritual freedom.

Okay, that's by the way. That's a message for another day. My point here is that:

---

*The gate you passed through to come to this world has a lot of influences on you. There are things - some good and some bad - it can deposit in your life. We need to discover the negative ones and prayerfully renounce them.*

---

That people can inherit problems or blessings from their lineages is a fact. In medicine, for example, doctors agree that illnesses can be passed on from one generation to the other, so they sometimes ask for the health history of your family to know how to administer the correct treatment.

Two powerful instruments confer on a person the right of membership of a particular family. These instruments are **BLOOD** and **NAME**. For example, by the combined work of the Blood and the Name of Jesus Christ, we become members of God's family. Because we also carry the blood and name of the family we come from we can share from the blessings or weaknesses from the family.

I know you're probably thinking, *"But I'm born again now, and all things have become new."* And I say yes, you're right. But did you disown the family from where you came into existence because you are now born again?

You see, getting born again does not cancel *the law of inheritance*; it instead gives us the power to reject negative inheritances and command positive ones to manifest. Let's see some Biblical examples of the power of generational blessings or curses.

## WHO MADE SARAH BARREN?

How did Sarah become barren? Who made her barren? Was it God?

Let's see what the Bible says...

The father of Abraham, Terah, was an idolater. He and his forefathers worshipped idols. The Bible says: *And Joshua said to all the people, Thus says the Lord God of Israel: 'Your fathers, **including Terah, the father of Abraham** and the father of Nahor, dwelt on the other side of the River in old times; and they served other gods.- Joshua 24:2*

His fathers had children early, but he was seventy years old before he had a child. Genesis 11:18-26 says:

> *18 Peleg lived thirty years and begot Reu.*

> *20 Reu lived thirty-two years and begot Serug.*

> *22 Serug lived thirty years and begot Nahor.*

> *24 Nahor lived twenty-nine years and begot Terah.*

> *26 Now Terah lived seventy years and begot Abram...*

What happened? Why did Terah's grandpas have children in their 30s while he waited until 70 to be able to have children?

Well, the Bible gives no clue. But if you agree that nothing happens without a cause, then we may be able to conjure a few conventions.

First, Terah, Abraham's father, was the fourth generation of his family. It's highly likely that the consequences of generational idolatry were beginning to manifest in the family, thus producing spiritual delays to expectations, health issues, and other unmentioned sufferings (See Numbers 14:18, Deut. 5:9). Secondly, there is also a possibility that Terah disobeyed the laws of his father's gods and got punished by the demons in charge of that worship. If you have interacted with people involved in Satanism, you'll know that they are always worried about punishments. Who knows, the demons behind the idols of their family may have punished him for some form of stubbornness or the other.

Okay, whatever the case, we know that Terah's delay in having children was not ordinary. There was a cause. And this cause also affected his children, especially his first son, Abraham.

In fact, Terah had a lot of family difficulties during his time. Haran, his son, the father of lot, died while he was still alive. That's very uncommon. His daughter-in-law, Sarai, became barren.

There is nowhere you will read in the Bible that God made Sarah barren. The spirit of barrenness passed on from Terah to Abraham, affecting his wife, Sarah. His father did not have children until seventy. And he reached seventy-five and had not seen anything. God came in only to help, deliver, and show him a perfect way out of the many ordeals of his life – A NEW COVENANT superior to the one his family had with other gods.

Did you also notice that in all of Abraham's 75 years in his homeland, the Bible did not record that he was a wealthy man? In Genesis Chapter 12 he received a call from God to be disconnected from the idolatry of his family line. Then in Chapter 13, he became very rich in cattle, in silver, and in gold (Gen. 13:2).

Abraham located his blessings as soon as he was disconnected from the evil inheritances, ancestral connections, and curses in his family. The process for his spiritual and physical establishment began the moment he accepted the Covenant of God Almighty. The same way, many people will locate their blessings when they are completely disconnected from the evil inheritances, connections, and curses in their lineages, and are aligned in the covenant of God Almighty through Jesus Christ.

The message is this: ***certain problems, marital issues, sicknesses, and habits can be passed on from past generations to the present.*** When seeking and praying for deliverance from certain situations, and they seem to refuse to go, do a more in-depth examination to see if the problem existed in your past generations – either from your mother or father side. This will enable you to pray the right prayers for deliverance.

## ANCESTRAL COVENANTS

*Now there was a famine in the days of David for three years, year after year; and David inquired of the Lord. And the Lord answered, "It is because of Saul and his bloodthirsty house because he killed the Gibeonites." - 2 Samuel 21:1*

Who were the Gibeonites? How did their killing become a reason for the problem in Israel?

Some five hundred years earlier, Joshua had entered into a solemn agreement with the Gibeonites. After the destruction of Jericho and Ai, the people of Gibeon sent representatives to trick Joshua and the Israelites into making a pact with them. The Gibeonites presented themselves as diplomats from a far, influential nation. Without consulting the high priests, Israel entered into a mutual covenant with them. Joshua later realized he had been deceived, but kept the pledge with the Gibeonites to let them live; however, he cursed and enslaved them as woodcutters and water-carriers.

Saul, in his zeal to the children of Israel and Judah - under the pretense of rigorous and faithful execution of the Canaanites - killed the Gibeonites, thereby breaking the pact that Joshua had with them some five hundred years earlier. His action brought a curse on the Israelites. Their lands became unproductive, and hunger ravaged the land. David, under whose reign the suffering began decided to seek the face of God. He prayed a prayer of inquiry and God revealed what the cause was and what they must do.

Notice that it was Saul who committed the offense. In his unguided zeal, he slew the Gibeonites – the descendants of ammonites – who had made a covenant of peace with the elders of Israel many years ago. But the consequences and sufferings reached down to the innocent citizens and generations. Why?

*Anointing does not cancel law and order.*

Ancestral covenants can be a reason for one's problems in life. It created a situation of famine, drought, scarcity – that is more like financial problems – for the Israelites. Until David took specific steps to deal with the circumstances, they suffered its consequences.

There may be some unpronounced, unknown, covenants in your family line that is speaking negatively against family members in one way or the other. Unless deliberate steps are taken to correct these ancient errors, wrong and idolatrous covenants through intentional renewal prayers, they will remain open doors for certain weaknesses and sufferings to continue to happen in a person's life or a family.

## NEGATIVE STRONGHOLDS IN THE FAMILY

A negative stronghold is a set of belief patterns or habits that are not right, but which one is not able to easily break away from. These beliefs, habits, and perceptions struggle with us and continually serve as leeway for the devil and his demons to continue to afflict us.

Until the roots of these negative strongholds are discovered and brought under the light of the Blood of Jesus Christ, one may continue to struggle with them, unable to break free.

For example, in Genesis 12:13, Abraham told lies about his wife. Through this action, a lying spirit entered his family lineage. Isaac also told lies about his wife (Gen. 26:1 -11). Jacob, the third generation, became a master trickster; and the children of Jacob - the fourth generation - not only told lies and cheated, but they also sold their blood brother into slavery. The sin gradually grew wings.

One can inherit a bad habit (such as alcoholism, anger, sexual pervasion, irrational fear, lying and trickery, fraudulent tendencies, and so on) from his parents or ancestors. Usually, it will be tough for the person to get rid of this habit no matter the psychological efforts and willpower exerted. It is only through thorough spiritual recognition and renunciation of these habits that the powers behind them are broken.

Have you ever wondered how a man of God such as David could succumb to the sin of adultery? Well, consider this: he was a descendant of Rahab, the professional harlot.

> *Salmon begot Boaz by Rahab, Boaz begot Obed by Ruth, Obed begot Jesse, and Jesse begot David the king-* Matthew 1:5-6

No doubt, this left a weakness in the family line, and would later develop wings by David's adultery. Amnon, David's oldest son, raped his half-sister, Tamar, committing incest, an abomination before God (2 Sam. 13:11 - 14). Absalom killed Amnon, in revenge for Tamar's rape and became the eldest son of David. He would later break every record in sexual perversion by sleeping with ten women at once (2 Sam 16: 21 -22). Adonijah, another son of David, died because of a woman (1 Kings 2:17 -25). Solomon, too, despite his wisdom and wealth, was not free from sexual lust. He married a whole city and befriended equally another town of women. And this led to his downfall.

Indeed, harmful habits can be inherited from parents or grandparents.

Have you ever seen a family where the father has a problem with overwhelming anger, his son appears to have been 'handed it,' and the grandfather had the same problem? Or have you noticed that not only do you hurt from something such as insistent, irrational fears or depression, but your mother and her father also suffered from it as well?

Those are effects produced by inherited curses. They are beyond learned behaviors; they are bondages that must be consciously broken with prayer.

Another example of typical symptoms of ancestral curses is family illnesses that seem to walk from one person down to the next, frequent financial difficulties, mental problems, persistent ridiculous fears and depression, and so on.

## A Prayer of Enquiry

Sometimes we need to spend time praying a prayer of inquiry than we spend begging God to do things for us. A prayer of inquiry is, *"Holy Spirit, please show me what I need to do. Show me what is responsible for this situation and guide me on the right way to pray through and obtain deliverance."*

Then we wait on the Lord until we can discern what to do. That is the key to deliverance. The Bible says:

*Call to Me, and I will answer you, and tell you [and even show you] great, and mighty things, [things which have been confined and hidden], which you do not know and understand and cannot distinguish (Jer.33:3 - AMP)*

A prayer of inquiry will adequately arm you with the right wisdom to pray and obtain answers to your prayers.

## 5. The Curse Of Wicked Men And Women

When I was building a house for my mum many years ago, we observed a lot of strange things on the property. I lived in Lagos, was sending money bit by bit to the contractor while my mum was supervising the project. Usually, when the contractor exhausts the money I posted, he would hold on until I was able to raise more money to send for work to continue.

Often my mum would visit the building site and see charms planted in different corners of the land. When she sees them, she would call me and narrate what she saw. I would pray with her and assure her that God is in control. Then she would invite people who would help her remove the charms. After a few days, she would visit the site and see other types of charms planted again. It got so bad that she became so scared of visiting the site.

Apparently, these charms were not planted there by spirits; neither did they fall from the sky. Human beings with evil intentions lodged them there.

The Bible says:

***The heart is deceitful above all things, and desperately wicked: who can know it?*** – Jer. 17:9

***'For from within, out of the heart of men, proceed evil thoughts, adulteries, fornications, murders.'*** - Mark 7:21

There are human beings whose minds are so twisted by the devil that they hate the wellbeing of others. These people go to any length to try to create spiritual frustrations, setbacks, sufferings, and illnesses for their targets. Through witchcraft, voodoo, sorcery, occultism, or other wicked works, they strive to harm their targets. Problems created by these types of people are what I classify as curses from evil men.

> *Now please come, curse these people for me, for they are too powerful for me; perhaps I will be able to defeat them and drive them out of the land. For I know [your reputation] that he whom you bless is blessed, and he whom you curse is cursed." – Number 22:6 (AMP)*

In this scripture, Balak, the king of Moab wanted to overrun the Israelites and prevent them from passing through his country to their Promised Land. But he had heard how God fought for them and knew that his military force might not be enough to defeat them. He needed to go spiritual.

He, therefore, hired Balaam, a popular prophet-diviner, to curse the Israelites. He knew that as long as they were under a powerful curse or spell, it would be easy to run them over and prevent God's plans for them.

Curses, arrows, attacks and evil projections from human beings with evil intentions can create spiritual weight and barriers for their victims, and cause them a lot of sufferings, prevent them from experiencing a breakthrough, and manifest the blessings of God for their lives. These are realities that the Bible corroborates; one that we see happening every day.

***Indeed they shall surely assemble, but not because of Me. Whoever assembles against you shall fall for your sake. …***

***No weapon formed against you shall prosper, and every tongue which rises against you in judgment you shall condemn. This is the heritage of the servants of the Lord, and their righteousness is from me, says the Lord*** *(Isaiah 54:15, 17)*

The Bible says they will gather. Yes, there are agents of evil who may gather and try to harm their perceived obstacles with witchcraft, curses, and other kinds of wicked activities. The Bible recognizes that these kinds of wickedness are rampant on earth. But we have the assurance of victory as we present these situations before the Lord and demand His justice in prayers.

## 6. The Curse Of The Law

*All who rely on observing the law are under a curse, for it is written: 'Cursed is everyone who does not continue to do everything written in the Book of the Law.' Clearly no one is justified before God by the law, because, 'the righteous will live by faith.' The law is not based on faith; on the contrary, 'The man who does these things will live by them.' Christ redeemed us from the curse of the law by becoming a curse for us, for it is written: 'Cursed is everyone who is hung on a tree'*
(Gal. 3:10-13 - NIV).

The curse of the law is the punishment imposed for not keeping the Law. The **Book of the Law** denotes the covenant laws that God made with the Israelites during the time of Moses. There were over 600 of these laws that the Jews had to keep to be right in God's eyes. The breaking of even one commandment placed a person under the punishment. The Law pointed out where we failed and fell short of God's will, but did not make us righteous.

Trying to realize salvation through obedience to the Law was impossible. The Apostle Paul tells us in Galatians

3:10 that everyone who does not keep the Law perfectly is cursed by it. The reason is that no one can comply with the Law correctly. For example, we all regularly break the first and ultimate commandment by failing to love God with all our spirit, soul and strength (Matthew 22:37–38).

The Law demands perfection—an impracticality because we're all sinful (Romans 3:23). As an outcome, all who try to live by the Law were under a divine curse. But the message is that Jesus *"redeemed us from the curse of the law by becoming a curse for us"* (Galatians 3:13).

Jesus Christ made the final sacrifice on the cross when He bore God's curse (Romans 3:25–26). Christ took the curse of the law on our behalf so that the righteousness of God could fall on us, even though we d not deserve it.

The curse of the law is no longer active once we acknowledge and accept that Jesus Christ as our Lord and Savior, confess our sins, and receive Him into our lives.

## The Bottom Line

There are many types of curses and many things that can constitute as roots of silent sufferings, frustrations, demonic questions, and so on. But the message is that there is deliverance in Jesus Christ. His blood and name are enough to give us perfect healing, deliverance and restoration from the problems happening as a result of curses.

# Chapter 3: Signs Of Curses And Spells

*I call heaven and earth as witnesses today against you, that I have set before you life and death, blessing and cursing; therefore choose life, that both you and your descendants may live* – Deut.30:19

Curses produce the opposite of blessings. The book of Deuteronomy chapter 28:15-68 enumerates some things that happen as a result of curses. These are the things that signal that one is under some form of a curse or the other:

- **Emotional instability**, constant fear, living in confusion

- **Inability to commit to plans**, often unreliable, flaky attitude, living aimlessly.

- **Recurring, hereditary family sicknesses**, health problems traced to other members of the family and relatives, past or present.

- **Prone to wounds**, always having lingering, chronic injuries, accidents, wounds, bruises, cuts, sores, boils.

- **Infertility problems** often found to also happen to other members of the family, such as barrenness, impotence, erectile dysfunction, female issues – such as continual unexplainable infections, hormone problems, menstrual problems, PMS, cramps, fibroids, painful sex, barrenness, miscarriages, cysts, tumors, bladder problems, kidney stones, etc.

- **Unusual marital problems**, such as severe delays in finding a spouse, family divides, divorce, polygamous tendencies, inability to settle down in marriage, moving from one partner to another too frequently, an unprecedented series family crisis from time to time, rebellious children, etc.

- **Overpowering Sexual Immorality,** such as incest, bestiality (sex with animals), addiction to pornography, sodomy (lesbianism and homosexuality), adulterous tendencies, especially when traced also to have happened with other members of the family, past or present.

- **Generational sins**, such as lying, fraudulent tendencies, alcoholism, practicing sexual pervasion for which one is not able to break free no matter how one innocently tries.

- **Unjustifiable financial lack,** working so hard but earning so little, inability to produce (Deuteronomy 28:17, 29), continual financial crisis for which there is no justifiable reason, unable to find favor with people, always having disappointment at the brink of breakthrough, having to work so hard with no commensurate results, always being taken advantage of – in the workplace, business dealings, and so on, not making tangible progress despite all your efforts.

- *Debtorcracy* (Deuteronomy 28:47-48), that is, being a slave to borrowing and debts, unable to get out of debt no matter how the person tries, not able to account for monies given or received, uncontrollable squandering and wasting of resources before realizing what is happening, addicted to get-rich-quick schemes, etc.

- **Severe low self-esteem** (Deuteronomy 28:43-44) often as a result of abuse, being spoiled, betrayed, or fear. Losing internal freedom to be oneself, can't make own decisions, always afraid to speak out, even when used and abused, always feeling and living like a caged person.

- **Prone to hate**, people just hate the person for no apparent reason, always getting punished for offenses they didn't commit, and so on.

- **Persistent nightmares and dreams,** such as consistently seeing oneself in the water or rivers in dreams, always being chased and struggling to survive in dreams, regularly having cats and dogs related dreams, consistently dreaming and seeing oneself in old places, ruins, mother's or father's ancestral homes, always writing exams in dreams or always seeing oneself in former school settings.

Usually when these kinds of dreams are repeated over and over and over, irrespective of one's prayers to stop them, then a more in-depth search is required. Most likely, a curse is responsible for the situation.

Additionally, if you suspect that something is wrong somewhere, but you can't lay hold of what it is exactly, then there may be a curse in operation. Usually, a curse can create a feeling of a cloud of darkness over your life; a sense of prayers is hitting the wall and not breaking through despite so many prayers and fasting.

# Chapter 4: Getting Rid of Curses and Spells

*How God anointed Jesus of Nazareth with the Holy Spirit and with power, who went about doing good and healing all who were oppressed by the devil, for God was with Him. - Acts 10:38*

As I said earlier, the message of this book is not just about the problem – that is, curses and their fruits. The news is about the solution – deliverance and freedom in Jesus Christ.

If you suspect that a situation you're struggling with right now has to do with curses, here are steps recommended to obtain deliverance ASAP.

# 1. Surrender Your Life to Christ

*The Lord is not slack concerning His promise, as some count slackness, but is longsuffering toward us, not willing that any should perish but that all should come to repentance. - 2 Peter 3:9*

As a minister, I've seen hundreds of people embark on prayers for deliverance from curses, and nothing happens at the end. I've seen people organize tens and tens of family deliverance prayers; they spend a lot of money, invite men of God to their ancestral homes for prayers, but after that, nothing happens. They buy anointing oils, carry anointed sands, and apply holy waters, yet nothing changes. Before you know it, they're looking for another prophet or man of God to pray for them again. After months and months of believing that this new prophet's prayers will change things, they see no changes. Then they go searching for another man of God for prayers again. And on and on, the circle continues.

Friend, there's no shortcut to deliverance. You can't buy it with money. You can't earn it by investing and sowing seeds to support the work of God. You only obtain it by the Blood of Jesus Christ. You receive it by repenting from your sins and committing your life to Christ.

---

*God has promised to deliver us from all oppressions of the devil, I mean, all of them – whether they be curses, sicknesses, financial lack, marriage problems, infertility, and so on.*

---

He can keep His promises to us. However, the first step to true and lasting deliverance and freedom is individual repentance and accepting Jesus Christ as Lord and Savior. You can't use someone else's repentance for your own freedom. No. God doesn't work that way. You must repent and accept Him. Then you can demand your deliverance.

People want deliverance, they want change, and they search for it desperately, but they don't want to repent of their sins and accept Christ as Lord and Savior. Too bad. They want what only God can give, but don't want to take how God wants to give it.

Well, the first step to freedom from curses is to accept Jesus Christ as your Lord and personal savior. I'm not talking about going to church. No. Many people go to church but don't know God. You can be going to church but not living for God. You can be going to church but not born again. So what I'm saying is repenting from your sins and striving to live a holy life unto the Lord.

What many people are doing today is coming to God and saying: *"Lord, please I need deliverance, here's some money for it. Take this money and give me relief. I'm very busy right now, so I can't give you my life. I've got other things to do with it."*

Unfortunately, it's not working. And it will never work that way.

If you need deliverance, come to God in humility, accept Jesus Christ as your Lord and personal savior, repent of your sins and begin to live for God. That's the first step to deliverance.

## 2. Understand that No Cause, No Curse

*Like a flitting sparrow, like a flying swallow, so a curse without cause shall not alight* - Proverbs 26:2

Always remember that a curse will not stand if there is no cause. So curses are only able to operate because they are holding on to something somewhere. Discovering these things is the first step to freedom. As a reminder, here are some things that can be a conduit for curses in one's life or family:

- Disregarding God's leading consistently

- Ancestral covenants (often unidentified until one asks serious questions)

- Dishonoring parents

- Constant use of foul, negative words over self

- Witchcraft projections (evil-minded individuals using satanic powers to create harm and pain

- Pornography

- Adultery and sexual pervasion

- Consulting witch doctors, spiritists, voodoo, fortunetellers, palm readers, etc

- Willfully committing fraud

- Being involved in the occult, freemason, lodge, Eckankar, Rosci cruces, Hare Krishna, etc

- Being involved with false religious organizations that do not accept the Deity of Christ – Jesus is the only way to God.

- Keeping statues, graven images, and accursed figurines (dolls) in one's home

- Having too many pictures of dead people around. There's nothing wrong with memorial photos, but having images of the dead all over the house connotes shrine.

- Financial unfaithfulness

- Occult books, covenanted rings, objects used in witchcraft, satanic movies, and even objects.

- Having hands laid on you by deceitful, fake prophets, or preachers who have compromised their faith in Christ, who have gone into mermaid worship, spiritism, and other forms of occult practices so that they can see visions. Yes, you may not know that these people have left the faith; you may not know they are using occult powers to spread their messages. But it doesn't cancel the fact that when they lay hands on you, they are not imparting the Spirit of God, but demonic spirits. Their spiritual impartation in you will be a doorway for demons to work against you. That is why God's word tells us to test every spirit and not run up and down looking for visions and prophecies.

- Soul ties and unhealthy relationships, such as unscriptural, unsupported business agreements, sexual relations with demonically possessed people, etc.

Before you start praying for deliverance from curses, ask yourself what might be the foundation for the evil in your life or family. And be bold enough to discuss and remove anything that might be a link to the curses. If they are specific sins, confess them and repent. If they are relationships and soul ties, break free from them and re-commit your life to Christ. If they are materials and objects, ask for wisdom and deal with them. If they are anger, unforgiveness, and bitterness, receive grace to make amends.

The Bible says:

*Many who had believed now came forward, confessing and disclosing their deeds. And a number of those who had practiced magic arts brought their books and burned them in front of everyone. When the value of the books was calculated, it came to fifty thousand drachmas. So the word of the Lord powerfully continued to spread and prevail-* **Acts 19:18-20**

Deliverance comes through reflection to identify the causes of what's happening and depending on God for help in dealing with these things. So take some time for reflection and praying a prayer of inquiry. Once you're able to discern the sources of the problems, you're halfway solving them.

The cause must be dealt with for the curse to be broken.

It's also possible that you're not able to completely figure out some of the causes of the curses in your life or family. But you're sure that the kind of problems you're going through is a curse in operation. In a situation like that, come before the Lord with an open heart and trust His deliverance in your life.

## 3. Pray Until You're Free

Deliverance from curses is not going to be a one day stuff, because curses are one of the most stubborn spiritual weights to deal with. So just like the woman in Luke chapter 18, you have to press hard for justice until justice is done.

Usually, when you've obtained deliverance, you'll know. The problem will stop, or you'll have an inner assurance that, yes, the situation is now under control.

If the problems don't stop immediately, but you have the assurance in your spirit that the situation is now under control, then switch to praise, because, come what may, the physical signs will eventually align to the spiritual victory you've obtained. Sometimes, too, your dreams will change; you will begin to have dreams of victory, blessings, and prosperity, as against your old dreams of nightmares and evil manipulations.

> *Until you obtain total deliverance and victory, with practical proof, don't stop praying.*

However, don't take this to mean that you must continue to run from pillar to post having people lay hands on you, receiving all manner of visions. That's not what I'm saying.

There are many Christians today who are occupied, running to and fro, looking to break curses off their lives that they are no longer living. Today, they are consulting this man of God, the next day, they are elsewhere. They keep going from place to place, doing all manner of family deliverance or the other. This is not a right way to live.

You should spend time seeking the Lord and praying targeted prayers until God's power is revealed in the situation. The Bible says, *"Deliver yourself like a gazelle from the hand of the hunter, and like a bird from the hand of the fowler"* (Proverbs 6:5).

Yes, deliver yourself.

Where necessary, you may seek prayer support, but the deliverance you do not give yourself first will not come from elsewhere. One thing is sure, as you sincerely and genuinely seek the Lord, He will set you free.

## 4. The Power Fasting

Fasting is a key to the impossible. Many difficult problems and situations in the Bible were addressed with 'FASTED' PRAYER. Jesus said that some demonic issues could only be fixed by fasting and prayer (Matthew 17:21). I believe that deliverance from curses and evil covenants are one of those situations.

As you get ready to pray against curses and evil covenants against your life and family, it is recommended that you fast with praying. Fasting to break free from spiritual bondage and limitations is highly recommended in scriptures. The Bible says:

*"Is not this the kind of fasting I have chosen: to loose the chains of injustice and untie the cords of the yoke, to set the oppressed free and break every yoke?* – **Isaiah 58:6**

Fasting will also increase your spiritual sensitivity to perceive what God will be leading you to do. *While the believers were fasting and praying, the Holy Spirit spoke* (Acts 13:2-3). As you fast and pray, pay attention to the leading of the Holy Spirit in your heart. Also, pay attention to your dreams. Whatever the Lord inspires you to deal with, ask for His grace and deal with it.

## 5. The Power of the Holy Communion

*As for thee also, by the blood of thy covenant I have sent forth thy prisoners out of the pit wherein is no water* (Zechariah 9:11)

The Blood of Jesus Christ is the seal of the new covenant. Under it, there's nothing hidden that will not be made known. His Blood invokes our deliverance and establishes us in God's presence.

While praying for deliverance from curses, one way to spiritually disconnect yourself from all forms of evil covenants and establish your union in the covenant of the Blood of Jesus Christ is continually using the symbol of the Holy Communion.

*Then Jesus said to them, 'Most assuredly, I say to you, unless you eat the flesh of the Son of Man and drink His blood, you have no life in you.' - **John 6:53***

*For as often as ye eat this bread, and drink this cup, ye do shew the Lord's death till he come. - **1 Cor. 11:26**.*

Apart from waiting to take the Holy Communion in Church service, you can prepare this spiritual meal and use it to minister deliverance and healing to yourself. Yes, you can take the Holy Communion personally as a way to spiritualize your unity and connection to Christ's death and resurrection. Then use the exercise to claim your translation from the kingdom of darkness to the kingdom of light, claim your healing, physical body restoration, and deliverance from curses and evil covenants.

Sometimes when the devil attacks my body or that of any member of my family, we use the anointing oil to pray and take the Holy Communion for our healing and deliverance. We do it every day until our deliverance manifest, and all glory goes to God Almighty.

I highly encourage you to prepare the communion and take every night after praying for deliverance. The Blood of Jesus Christ will set you free.

## 6. The Power of the Anointing Oil

*Is anyone among you sick? Let him call for the elders of the church, and let them pray over him, anointing him with oil in the name of the Lord. And the prayer of faith will save the sick, and the Lord will raise him up. And if he has committed sins, he will be forgiven.* – **James 5:14-15**

One night as we were all asleep, our one-year-old daughter, Annabel, suddenly started crying. She cried and cried and would not stop. We did everything humanly possible to stop her from crying, but she did not. We wanted to rush her to the hospital, but it was in the middle of the night, so couldn't do much. So my wife and I decided to pray over her. We somehow felt she must have had a spiritual attack in the dream or so. Yes, children can also be attacked by the devil. They can also have nightmares and other spiritual issues that only prayer and counseling can resolve.

So we decided to pray for her. We prayed a prayer of agreement using a few scriptures that we always use to pray for children. After the agreement prayer with my wife, I carried her and asked my wife to go back to bed. I took her to the sitting room and began to anoint her and speak God's WORD over her life. Twenty minutes later, she stopped crying and slept off in my arms.

We may not know exactly what happened that night as she was just one-year-old and may never explain to us. But we obtained victory in the name of Jesus Christ, using spiritual tools the Lord has instructed us to use – a prayer of agreement and the anointing oil.

Ministering to ourselves with anointing oil is something we should all learn to do from time to time. The anointing oil is a symbol of the Holy Spirit used for consecration, healing, and enthronement. During your prayer rounds to break curses, always anoint yourself after a prayer session, and declare yourself dedicated and consecrated to the Lord. As a dedicated instrument to God, no demon has right over your life anymore.

## 7. How Long Should You Pray?

As I said earlier, pray until something happens. Pray until you're free. Pray until deep down in your heart an air of freedom wells up in you, until you have an unshakable assurance that it's done.

Start with a 3-day prayer circle. Then do another 7-day prayer round. Then another 14-day round, then a 21-day circle, then a 40-day round, etc. Don't stop, yes, don't stop, until you're free.

Always bear in mind that the devil, his demons, and whatever they are carrying out in your life or family at the moment have the ultimate goal of frustrating, killing and destroying you (John 10:10). But Jesus wants you to have life and have it more abundantly. He wants you to have a better life. Refuse anything contrary to that and continue to demand justice until justice is done.

## 8. When Should You Pray?

The three daily special times of prayer recorded in both the Old and New Testaments were explicitly the third hour, the sixth hour and the ninth hour of the day, or 9:00 A.M., 12 noon and 3:00 P.M. The Apostles observed them in the New Testament. However, they were not a part of the Law of Moses or Jesus Christ, and nowhere in the Bible is their compliance mandatory.

With the liberty we have in Christ, these times may be easily adapted or adjusted to fit your contemporary daily schedule. I have slightly modified these prayer times based on what works more effectively in deliverance experiences and scriptural insights. So here are the times we recommend that you select from and pray for your deliverance...

- 12:00am – 1:00am (Midnight Session)
- 3:00 Am – 4:00 Am (Early Morning Session)
- 6:00am – 7:00am (Morning Session)
- 9:00 A.M. – 10:00 A.M – Third Hour Session
- 12:00 – 1:00 pm (Midday or Sixth Hour Session)

- 3:00 pm – 4:00 pm (Afternoon or Ninth hour Session)

- 9:00pm – 10:00pm (Night Session)

You may choose any of these sessions and pray for your chosen number of days. There are no mandates, which means you could chose afternoon session today and pray, and chose midnight session tomorrow and pray. Whatever is convenient for your schedule is welcome.

However, we always recommend the midnight and early morning sessions. For some mysterious reasons, the night hours provides a better atmosphere for earnest warfare prayers. And yes, what happens in the night can drastically influence the results of the day. The Bible says:

*You will not fear the terror of night, nor the arrow that flies by day - **Psalm 91:5***

*But while men slept, his enemy came and sowed tares among the wheat, and went his way. – **Matt.13:25***

*Everyone who does evil hates the day, and will not come into the light for fear that their deeds will be exposed - **John 3:30**.*

*Do not desire the night, when people are cut off in their place. - **Job 36:20***

All these scriptures are explicitly saying that the night hours serve as cover-ups for many evils. David said in Psalm 119:62, *"At midnight I will rise to give thanks to You, because of Your righteous judgments."* As a prophet, he knew the power of midnight prayers. As he prayed in those times, he saw God's righteous judgments on his enemies. You'll want to do the same thing if you desire quick judgments on all your oppression.

The Bible says in Exodus 12:29 that *"at midnight the LORD smote all the firstborn in the land of Egypt, from the firstborn of Pharaoh that sat on his throne unto the firstborn of the captive that was in the dungeon; and all the firstborn of cattle."* At midnight Paul and Silas prayed and sang praise unto the Lord, and an angel freed them (Acts 16:25).

Use the midnight hours like Samson to uproot the gates of your enemy. Prayers to dislodge evil powers, obtain deliverance from curses, and break demonic covenants are best done in the night hours, especially from

Midnight to 6:00 A.M. Praying at this time gives you the needed concentration and focus to destroy whatever the enemies have disseminated, and release your stolen blessings.

## Let's Recap

How do you get rid of curses?

1. You need to be born again and surrender your life to Christ. You need to repent of every sin and dedicate your life to live holy to the Lord.

2. Prayerfully seek to understand the causes of the curses. There's always something responsible for why something is happening.

3. Persist in prayers. Don't accept anything other than perfect freedom. Pray until you're free, and know it.

4. Seek your deliverance with fasting

5. Continually apply the mystery of the Holy Communion in your prayers

6. Constantly use the mystery of the anointing oil in your prayers.

7. Pray more in the night hours

8. Believe that as you pray, your prayers will be answered

# Chapter 5: Prayers to Destroy Curses and Spells

*Therefore I say to you, whatever things you ask when you pray, believe that you receive them, and you will have them.* - Mark 11:24

There are many prayers below, arranged under different headings. These prayers are to be guides. When you read a prayer, calm down and use your own words to pray the point until you're soaked in its message. No matter how long you've been suffering, these prayers will bring deliverance in a matter of days. Choose one or two prayers for a day and pray the prayers in any one of the following ways:

1. Pray for three straight nights, always starting at the midnight hour.

2. Pray for seven consecutive nights, always beginning at the midnight hour

3. Pray for fourteen straight nights, always starting at the midnight hour

4. Pray for twenty-one successive nights, always starting at the midnight hour

5. Fast for three days, praying at intervals in the day and breaking the fast at 3 pm, or 6 pm.

6. Fast for seven days, praying at intervals in the day and breaking the fast at 3 pm, or 6 pm.

7. Fast for fourteen days, praying at intervals in the day and breaking the fast at 3 pm, or 6 pm.

8. Fast for twenty-one days, praying at intervals in the day and breaking the fast at 3 pm, or 6 pm (Daniel Fast).

# Prayer 1: A Prayer of Praise and Thanksgiving

*Be anxious for nothing, but in everything by prayer and supplication, with thanksgiving, let your requests be made known to God* **- Philippians 4:6**

Even though you want to pray for deliverance, it's important to begin your prayer with serious praise and thanksgiving. Yes, all prayers must be mixed with thanksgiving and praise. Thank God for the gift of prayer, thank Him for His promise to answer your prayer, even before you pray. Spend time singing, worshipping and declaring these prayers of thanks to God

**PRAYER**

*Heavenly Father, I thank You because You have been on my side all along. If not for You, Lord, I would have been consumed and forgotten. Your grace and power have kept me safe and protected me from the plans of the devil and those who rise against me.*

*Even in my unrighteousness and backslidden times, Lord, Your righteousness has kept me. You have not allowed the enemy to succeed over me. I praise You forever and ever, in Jesus name.*

---

*O Lord, I thank You for I am fearfully and wonderfully made; wonderful are Your works, and my soul knows it very well.*

*I thank You for saving my soul from hell. I thank You for making me Your child. I thank You for establishing me in Your covenant of grace through the Blood of Jesus Christ. Thank You for Your promise and gift of the Holy Spirit.*

*I thank You, Lord, for Your divine plan for my life.*

*I thank You for You have always intervened in my affairs. I praise You because, even now and forever, You will never leave me nor forsake me.*

*Even when I feel that my suffering and pain is too much and that You are not answering my prayers, Lord, I know that You are bringing me to a place of spiritual maturity and more in-depth understanding of*

*Your ways. I know that Your love and compassion for me will never fail. For this, I say thank You, Lord. In Jesus name.*

---

*Heavenly Father, I show appreciation to You for everything You have done for me in the past. I thank You for everything You are doing in my life at the moment. And I thank You for everything You will do for me in the future.*

*I know that my future is secure in You. I know that You will always lift me up when I fall. I know You will cause my mind to stay in You and keep me in perfect peace. I know that You will cause everything and everyone, even those who oppose me at the moment, to work out for my own good.*

*Lord, I know that You will daily protect me from the snares of the fowler and the noisome pestilence. I know that Your angels are in charge over my life and family, fighting for me, and making me a conqueror.*

*For all these, I say thank You, Father, in Jesus name.*

*O Lord, I thank You for bringing me this far in You. Thank You for the past years of my life and thank You for this year. Thank You for sustaining me in Your love.*

*I bless Your name Lord for Your promise of total deliverance from all works of the devil. I praise Your name for guaranteeing my freedom from curses, witchcraft, evil attacks, spiritual delays, and sicknesses.*

*Thank You for giving me the opportunity to seek and find You in prayer, and meditation. Be praised forever, in Jesus name.*

---

*To You, O God of my forefathers, the God of Abraham, Isaac, and Jacob; the God who saves to the uttermost; I give You thanks and praise, for You have given me wisdom and might.*

*As I proceed in this season of praise, prayer, and warfare, Lord, I thank You in advance for my victory and breakthrough.*

*You, God, is the God of Israel, You are amazing in Your holy place, and gives strength and power to Your people. I thank You in advance for my total deliverance from all curses, and for supplying all my needs according to Your riches in Christ Jesus.*

---

*Lord, I enter into the gates of righteousness, freedom and deliverance, boldness, power and sound mind; I enter through them this day with thanksgiving, in Jesus name.*

*Amen!*

## Prayer 2: A Prayer of Repentance & Forgiveness

This is a critical session in the deliverance process. You need to spend time here and confess all known faults out. Read James 5:16 and speak up before the Lord, or the deliverance minister, any past lifestyles, attitudes, addictions, fears, sins, feelings, thoughts, and things you have done that may be a conduit for demonic operation in your life.

*If we confess our sins, he is faithful and just and will forgive us our sins and purify us from all unrighteousness* - 1 John 1:9

*He who covers his sins will not prosper, but whoever confesses and forsakes them will have mercy.* - Proverbs 28:13

The direct benefit of acknowledging and speaking out your past sins and lifestyles to the Lord and the deliverance minister is that you obtain mercy, while the consequence of refusing to divulge is a denial of answers to prayers.

Let me say this here. Only God delivers from curses and spells and all other problems. The deliverance minister has no power to offer deliverance or anything for that matter. He is just a medium through which God's power is released. And God, who owns the power, won't release it if His words are ignored.

So don't try to test the prophetic ability of the minister. Open up and let God move in your life. Use these prayers as a guide to repent and confess your faults to God.

## PRAYER

*Heavenly Father, I humble myself before You today and confess my sins. I acknowledge that I have walked in disobedience to Your leadings in the past, even to the present, and followed after my own ways. There are many times I let my desires, judgments, and human perceptions prevail in my relationship with You and others. There are many times I let my flesh decide for me what to do and how to live.*

*Today, O Lord, I confess all of these sins to You and ask for Your forgiveness. In particular, Lord, I pray for Your forgiveness over the following sins in my life:*

............................  ............................  ............................

**(Mention specific areas of your life that need to be brought open before the Lord)**

*Father, I am sorry for letting these sins rule my life. I confess them before Thee today and accept Your gift of forgiveness. Please give me the grace to overcome these sins and live for Thy glory from now onwards, in Jesus name.*

---

*Father Lord, I bring before You every soul tie, negative covenants, agreements, unholy relationships, and permissions that You did not sanction for me, but which is still existing in my life. I ask You to forgive me for entering into these ties, bonds, and relationships. By Your Holy Spirit, Lord, lead me out of these unions and help me to see Your light and walk out of them, in Jesus name.*

*Lord, I ask Thee for grace to forgive those who have sinned against me from the past through to this moment. I surrender to You any bitterness in my heart and ask for Your healing and restoration. I release all of the hurts and pains in my heart to You today and plead the Blood of Jesus Christ in my spirit, soul, and body.*

*I declare today that I completely forgive all those who have offended me; I release them from the captivity of bitterness in my heart.*

*Through the Blood and name of Jesus Christ, I reclaim every benefit, opportunity, and blessing that unforgiveness has delayed or denied in my life, in Jesus name.*

---

*O Lord, please touch the heart of those I have offended to forgive and forget my offenses. Give us the opportunity to amend our ways and follow after peace once again.*

*Father, if there are people I need to forgive for my life to breakthrough, please lead me to them now in Jesus name.*

---

*Dear Fire of the Holy Spirit, purge my heart of every unforgiveness, bitterness, regret, self-pity, low self-esteem, dwelling on the past, and vengeance thoughts, in Jesus name.*

---

*Today, O Lord, may every seed of unforgiveness and bitterness in my life be destroyed. By the Blood of Jesus Christ, I release myself from every form of captivity resulting from inherited family offenses, bitterness, quarrels, and fights, in Jesus name.*

---

*Father, Lord, I plead the Blood of Jesus Christ today over any sins committed by my parents and ancestors, from my mother and father side.*

*I state openly that these sins...*

**(...the sin of adultery, idolatry, murder, polygamy, spiritism, human sacrifice, agreements and covenants with demons, occultism, etc.).**

...are abomination before Thee and whatever evil consequences are upon us before now as a result of these sins, we are deserving of them.

But, Lord, I stand in the gap for my family today and ask for forgiveness for these sins. You said that You will overlook the days of ignorance and now command us to repent.

Lord, I repent on behalf of my family, and receive forgiveness on their behalf, in Jesus name.

---

Through the Sanctified Blood of Jesus Christ, I cancel any satanic covenants, agreements, connections, exchanges, vows, or transactions made over our lives, bodies, souls, and surroundings by our ancestors and early parents, in Jesus name.

*I declare that my family and I are redeemed from the hand of the devil by the precious Blood of Jesus Christ.*

*I declare that all satanic seats, altars, dominions, principalities, controls, rulers of darkness, spiritual soldiers of wickedness, and all demonic workings have no more authority or power over us, in Jesus name.*

---

*I declare today that the devil and his demons are forever denied access into our family, lives, and destinies. I raise a spiritual banner over my family today and decree that the Blood of Jesus Christ is speaking for us henceforth. We are walking in dominion, power, and God's prophetic purpose for our lives– in the name of Jesus Christ.*

---

*Thank You, Lord, for answering my prayers; thank You for the gift of forgiveness and healing that is now extended to me, my family, and ancestral lineage, in Jesus name.*

*Amen.*

# Prayer 3: A Prayer for Revelation and Understanding

*₁₆... making mention of you in my prayers: ₁₇that the God of our Lord Jesus Christ, the Father of glory, may give you the spirit of wisdom and revelation in the knowledge of Him, ₁₈ the eyes of your understanding being enlightened; that you may know what is the hope of His calling, what are the riches of the glory of His inheritance in the saints. -*
**Ephesians 1:16-18**

Apostle Paul prayed for the believers' eyes to be opened and enlightened. He prayed for them to have the revelation that will build their confidence and establish their faith in God.

Beloved, deliverance requires revelation. Not the one they use to get you to run after a man of God, but the one that God gives, directing you on areas to pray and what to address. We do not know exactly where to channel our prayers or how to pray. We may try, but we need God's guidance. So spend time and open up your heart and wait on the Lord for His direction. Use these prayers to seek God's guidance in your prayers for deliverance

## PRAYER

*Father I pray, open thou my eyes that I may behold wondrous things out of Thy Law. As I read or listen to Your Word, enlighten my heart, and give me specific leadings for my freedom, healing, restoration, and breakthrough, in Jesus name.*

---

*Cause me, O Lord, to hear Your voice telling me the way to pray, the way to go, and the way to respond to the situations in my life today, so that I may experience Your supernatural touch and blessings in every area of my life, in Jesus name*

---

*Father, Your Word says that the Holy Spirit will reveal to us things to come, He will teach us all things, and even bring to our remembrance what You have told us in the past. I pray today, Lord, through the Holy Spirit, teach me all that I need to know and do, even as I wait on You, to be totally free from the curses and spells working against my life and family before now, in Jesus name.*

---

*O Lord, show me everything I need to deal with in my life. Show me relationships I need to exit. Show me items in my possession that are not of You, that I need to do away with. Show me specific sins, attitudes, and deeds in my life that the devil is using as a leeway into my life, and help me, Lord, to deal with them as You want.*

*And, Lord, Give me new ideas that will establish Your plan for my life, bring glory to your name, and joy to Your people on earth, in Jesus name.*

---

*Lord, according to Jeremiah 33:3, You said that we should call on You in prayer and that You will answer and show us great and mighty things that we do not know.*

Many times when David enquired of You regarding a situation, You showed up and gave him clarity. You revealed to him exactly what to do. He would follow Your leading, and You would give Him victory.

Lord, You have not changed, for You are the same yesterday, today and forever. So I trust You completely to guide me in this situation to victory and breakthrough, and Your name will be glorified, in Jesus name.

---

Father Lord, if there are specific instructions and direction You gave me in the past which I disregarded, I ask You to forgive me, and set me free from the consequences of disobedience, in the name of Jesus Christ.

---

Lord, according to Your Word, a curse causeless shall not come. I know there is always something that a problem, a curse, or a situation, will hold as an open door to thrive. So I pray today, Lord, give me insight, revelation, and spiritual understanding so that I can *confront the situations I am praying about now from their roots, in Jesus name.*

---

*I unlock my spiritual eyes, ears, and senses today, and open the gate of my heart for God's direction, in the Mighty name of Jesus Christ.*

---

*I will no longer grope in darkness. I will no longer be blind spiritually. When I lie down to sleep, my dreams shall be ways for God's voice to me in Jesus name.*

---

*I bind all the evil powers that attack my dreams and make me blind to what God is saying, in Jesus name*

---

*From today, O Lord, I receive divine illumination concerning my life and destiny, in Jesus name.*

*Thank You, Lord for answered prayers,*

Amen.

# Prayer 4: A Prayer for Grace to Persist in Prayers

Luke chapter 18 tells the story of a widow who has been ill-treated. Day after day she brings her case before a judge who "neither feared God nor cared what people thought." The judge is at first uninterested in the widow's appeal, but then he is forced to review his position because she refuses to take "no" for an answer. He finally yields, saying to himself, "Even though I do not fear God or care what people think, but because this widow keeps troubling me, I will give her justice, so that she will not tire me down by her continual coming."

The message in this parable is not that God is like an insensitive judge who must be pestered to answer to our request, but that how much more will God, our good father, "bring around justice for His people, who cry out to Him day and night?"

Persistence forces us to the real center of prayer, which is not something but someone. It deepens our relationship with God and forces the heart to examine what it truly wants most.

Do you want God's deliverance? Then persist in prayers.

Use these prayers to receive grace to continue until your deliverance shows forth.

## PRAYER

*Lord, there are times that my heart faints and my mind raises many questions about the efficacy of prayer and Your love. Thank You, Lord, that in such times that I am weak, You remain my strength. Be glorified in Jesus name.*

---

*O Lord, is there anything in my life and family that the enemy has tampered with, harmed, or destroyed, in my times of weakness, spiritual laziness, anxiety, fear, confusion, and backsliding, O Lord, heal and restore me today, in Jesus name.*

---

*Today, O Lord, I claim back my confidence, faith, boldness and sound mind, in Jesus name.*

*Heavenly Father, baptize me with a spirit of persistence, a spirit that will never give up, a spirit that will continue to tarry in prayers until Your promises are fully revealed in my life, in Jesus name.*

*I declare today, O Lord, just like the woman in Jesus parable in Luke chapter 18, I will never give up. I will never stop praying. And I know that justice and divine intervention is guaranteed for me, in the gracious name of Jesus Christ.*

Amen.

## Prayer 5: A Prayer to Break Self-Inflicted Curses

*Heavenly Father, You said that the power of death and life is in the tongue; and that we will be justified or condemned by our words (Prov. 18:21, & Matt. 12:37). Lord, I know that Your Words are ever true. Heaven and earth will pass away but Your Words will not.*

*Lord, I acknowledge that I have used my words in ways that were not decent and pleasing to You. I have used my words to hurt others, speak negative things about my life, partner, children, family, and nation. Father, I now ask You to forgive all my wrong use of words from past to present, in Jesus name.*

---

*Blood of Jesus Christ, sanctify my tongue and purify my heart. Empower me to be a carrier and speaker of life, health, encouragement, and peace from today onwards, in Jesus name.*

*Whatever pain and hurt I have brought upon myself, my family, my career, my children, and my family, as a result of my wrong use of words in the past, Heavenly father, heal and restore me today, in Jesus name*

---

*In the name of Jesus Christ, I decree that no corrupt word will proceed out of my mouth henceforth, but what is good for edification, imparting grace to the hearers, health to the sick, and blessings to all, in Jesus name.*

---

*I willingly command myself to put away all forms of bitterness, wrath, anger, clamor, malice, and evil speaking from today. I command myself to be kind to others, tenderhearted, forgiving, and ever ready to be a blessing, in the name of Jesus Christ.*

---

*I break any curse I have imposed on myself ignorantly, through my use of negative words, anger, fear, and anxiety, in Jesus name.*

*It is written that the days of ignorance, the Lord overlooks (Acts 17:30). Therefore, if there are any evil happening in my life and family as a result of my negative confessions in the past, I command them to stop today.*

*I replace all self-inflicted pains and events in my life today with God's favor, peace and breakthrough, in Jesus name.*

---

*I bless myself from now onwards; I bless my home; I bless my career; I bless my family; I bless my church, and I bless my children.*

*Henceforth, my going out shall be a blessing and my coming back shall be a blessing. I shall be blessed in the city; I shall be blessed in the country.*

*When and where others are saying there is a casting down, I shall be saying there is a lifting up, in Jesus name.*

*O LORD, according to your Word in Romans 8:28, everything is working out for my good. I am a blessing to my family. I am a blessing to my country. I am a blessing to my generation. In the name of Jesus.*

# Prayer 6: A Prayer to Deal With Parental Curses

*Almighty Father, the maker of heaven and earth, creator of family and the home system, I come to You today with thanks. I appreciate Your wisdom in establishing the home system, through which Your purpose on earth is fulfilled. Be praised forever and ever, in Jesus name.*

---

*Today, O Lord, I thank You for my parents and guardians. I thank You for giving them the grace to bring me to this world. I thank You for enabling them to care for and protect my siblings and me over the years. Receive all the praise in Jesus name.*

---

*Dear Lord, I ask for forgiveness, in any way I have dishonored and disrespected my parents or guardians in the past. Father, I was ignorant. Please have mercy on me. Psalm 30:5 says that Your anger is but for a moment, Your favor is for life; weeping may endure for a night, but joy comes in the morning.*

*Father, in Your mercy and favor, remember me, in Jesus name.*

---

*Lord, I pray today that You heal and restore my relationship with my parents and guardians. Give me the grace to forgive them, in any way I feel they haven't treated me right in the past. As I take new steps to make amends with them, O Lord, may Your power prevail in our hearts, and may Your peace, love, and fear be established in our emotions once more, in Jesus name.*

---

*From this day, O Lord, I bring before the Blood of Jesus Christ every curse, negative words, and evil pronouncements from my parents, guardians, and teachers in the past. I receive deliverance from the consequences of these statements from today, in Jesus name.*

---

*Every spiritual door opened in my life, health, and family as a result of past pronouncements from my* parents, guardians and teachers, O Lord, I close them today, in Jesus name.

And I decree healing and restoration from every hurt and pain affecting our lives as a result of these past pronouncements, in Jesus name

---

Dear Holy Spirit, please uproot and flush out every seed of bitterness, malice and fighting in me and my parents. Let these evil seeds creating a distance between us be flushed out today, in Jesus name.

---

As a parent also, Lord, I pray that all curses, negative pronouncements and evil wishes, I have uttered or wished in the past, against my children and those under my care, be nullified today, in Jesus name.

---

Today, I exercise myself onto forgiveness and willfully forgive my children, grandchildren, and anyone whom I cared for in the past that offended me. I drop all burdens against every one of them, and release *everyone from whatever curse happening in their lives as a result of this harbored pain in my heart, in Jesus name.*

---

*I speak blessings and peace in the name of the Lord on my children, stepchildren, grandchildren and everyone connected to me. I decree that it shall be well with all of them in Jesus name*

---

*From this day forward, Lord, I proclaim my offspring blessed. I declare my generation blessed. I declare my family members blessed. I pronounce my home healed and blessed, in Jesus name.*

*Amen*

# Prayer 7: Prayers to Deal with The Curses Of Disobedience

*Dear Heavenly Father, King of kings and LORD of Lords, here am I today once again. I want us to talk about my stubbornness and disobedience to Your instructions in the past. Lord, as Your Word has said, disobedience is as a sin of witchcraft. And yes, Lord, I am guilty of this sin in many ways.*

*I can't even begin to count how many times I have disobeyed Your instructions in my heart, not paid attention enough to understand what You were saying, gone my ways and not bothered about what You want me to do regarding certain situations.*

*I know that many times, I have disobeyed you in my marital life, my relationships, decisions, money and healthy life.*

*Today, Lord, I ask for mercy and forgiveness, in Jesus name.*

*If the Lord counts our iniquities, no one will stand. Father, I'm not worthy to stand before You based on my obedience. Not at all. But I am standing before You today based on the complete and perfect obedience of Jesus Christ. Look upon me with pity and set me free from all the consequences of my past disobedience to Your instructions and leadings, in Jesus name.*

---

*According to Isaiah chapter 42:19-22, we are spoiled because we have heard and seen many things but not paid attention. Lord, help me to understand what I hear and see from today. Help me to easily and quickly discern Your voice and what You want me to do in them, in Jesus name.*

---

*Today, I commit myself to walk in obedience to God's voice in my heart. Lord, May I not be confused when You are speaking to me. Help me to know without a doubt that a particular thought, idea, or plan is of you or not of you. May I have the courage and confidence to reject anyone that is not of you and commit to the ones that are of You. And as I set myself to walk in*

*Your ways, I decree according to Isaiah 1:19 that I shall eat the good of the land, in the name of Jesus.*

---

*May every seed of disobedience in my heart and life die today, in Jesus name*

---

*I decree from today that I shall no longer labor in vain. My efforts and the work of my hands shall bear fruits. I shall be blessed in all that I do, in Jesus name.*

*Amen*

# Prayer 8: Prayer Against Ancestral And Inherited Curses

Begin this prayer session with intense praise and worship. Also, pray these prayers in the midnight. And reflect on the following scriptures. Read them out loud before you begin to pray.

**Jeremiah 31:28-30:** *Just as I watched over them to uproot and tear down, and to overthrow, destroy and bring disaster, so I will watch over them to build and to plant," declares the LORD. ₂₉ "In those days people will no longer say, 'The parents have eaten sour grapes, and the children's teeth are set on edge.' ₃₀ Instead, everyone will die for their own sin; whoever eats sour grapes--their teeth will be set on edge.*

**2 Corinthians 5:17:** *Therefore if any man is in Christ, he is a new creature: old things are passed away; behold, all things become new.*

**Galatians 3:13-14:** *Christ redeemed us from the curse of the law by becoming a curse for us, for it is written: 'Cursed is everyone who is hung on a pole.' He* *redeemed us so that the blessing given to Abraham might come to the Gentiles through Christ so that by faith we might receive the promise of the Spirit.*

## PRAYER

*Heavenly Father, once again, I bring the sins of my family tree before you. I confess all their sins, including stealing, polygamy, the killing of human beings, idolatry, slavery, sacrificing human beings to idols, demons, and Satan, eating human flesh and every evil and wicked act that they have done.*

*I plead the Blood of Jesus Christ on my family lineage, my father and mother side.*

*I ask for complete forgiveness of all these evils in Jesus name*

---

*By the Blood of Jesus Christ, O LORD, I break and nullify all curses, covenants, and initiations made by my ancestors or by myself in the air, earth, under the earth, in the waters above, or underneath the earth.*

*Because I am now in Christ Jesus, old things have passed away; all things have become new. Therefore, every form of childhood manipulation still working against my life, family, marriage, and destiny, be destroyed in Jesus name.*

---

*May the Blood of Jesus Christ flow through to my foundation and the entire design of my body system and cleanse me from all childhood defilements and evil inheritance.*

*I set myself free from every problem and difficulty operating in my life as a result of ignorant childhood initiation and evil practices by my parents, grandparents, and guardians, in Jesus name.*

---

*Every demonic seed deposited into my life and my body from my childhood, be roasted by fire in the name of Jesus.*

*According to the word of God, if a man is in Christ, he is a new creature, old things are passed away, and all things become new? I, therefore, announce this day before heaven and earth,*

**"I am a child of God. Jesus Christ is in my life. I have been removed from satanic kingdom and translated into the kingdom of light. I am a new creature, destined to succeed in everything I do. I cannot be stopped by anything.**

*Every curse holding onto the covenants of my ancestries to chase my life and destiny, you are now helpless. By the blood of Jesus Christ, I announce my total freedom from every one of you, in Jesus name.*

---

*I command all familiar spirits perpetrating evil in my life and family, hindering the glory of God from showing forth in our efforts, be crippled and get back into the abyss.*

*Every demonic shrine, altar, and temple existing in my life and family, be destroyed in the mighty name of Jesus Christ.*

*Today, O LORD, I command every satanic covering and cloud of darkness over my life and family to be utterly destroyed.*

*Every eater of flesh and drinker of bloood chasing my life and family, die by fire, in the name of Jesus Christ.*

---

**(Lay your hand on your belly and pray):**

*I break every evil chord connecting me to the curses on the ancestors of my family and community, in the name of Jesus Christ.*

---

*From today, O LORD, according to Mathew 18:18, I forbid untimely death, sickness, barrenness, disappointment, and failure in my life and family.*

*Let every closed door, lost opportunities, and gifts in my life and family, be restored, in Jesus name.*

## READ:

**2 Corinthians 6:14-17** - *Do not be unequally yoked together with unbelievers. For what fellowship has righteousness with lawlessness? And what communion has a light with darkness?*

*15 And what accord has Christ with Belial? Or what part has a believer with an unbeliever?*

*16 And what agreement has the temple of God with idols? For you are the temple of the living God. As God has said: 'I will dwell in them and walk among them.*

*I will be their God, and they shall be My people.' Therefore... 'Come out from among them and be separate, says the Lord. Do not touch what is unclean, and I will receive you.'*

**Colossians 1:13-14** - *He has delivered us from the power of darkness and conveyed us into the kingdom of the Son of His love, in whom we have redemption through His blood, the forgiveness of sins.*

## PRAY

*O LORD, as it is written in Colossians 1:13-14, I have been translated from the kingdom of darkness into the kingdom of the son, Jesus Christ.*

*In him, I have redemption, through His blood, even the forgiveness of sins. I, therefore, make the following proclamation today before heaven and earth.*

*I belong to a new kingdom, the kingdom of light.*

*I am seated with Christ in the heavenly places, far above all principalities and powers. Nothing can stop me from manifesting the glory of God; nothing will prevent me from being healed and walk in divine health.*

*In Jesus name.*

---

*I call upon the fire of God right now to destroy permanently every hidden and unknown curse, spell, charm, incantations and evil statements made against my life and family.*

*Every hidden covenant working against my life, family, and destiny be destroyed in Jesus name.*

*I now belong to a new covenant of life, peace, health, and prosperity sealed with the Holy blood of Jesus Christ*

---

*I decree today, whatever demonic instrument of accusation in my possession, knowingly or unknowingly, let their power be paralyzed in Jesus name.*

*I decree that I am completely delivered and FREE from any form of generational curse, covenant or restriction working against my life*

*It is written that whoever the Son sets free, is free indeed (John 8:36). Therefore, LORD, I decree that I am set free from ancestral curses and spells, in Jesus Name.*

*Amen.*

# Prayer 9: Prayers to Deal With Curses And Spells Of Wicked Men, Occultism, Witchcraft, and Evil-Minded Individuals

Begin this prayer session with intense praise and worship. Also, pray these prayers in the midnight. And reflect on the following scriptures. Read them out loud before you begin to pray.

**Psalm 91:1-16**

**Psalm 34:7** - The angel of the LORD encamps around those who fear him, and he delivers them

**Exodus 22:18** - Thou shalt not suffer a witch to live.

**Micah 5:11-12** - I will tear down your walls and demolish your defenses. I will put an end to all witchcraft, and there will be no more fortune-tellers.

**Micah 3:7** - Seers will be put to shame. Those who practice witchcraft will be disgraced. All of them will cover their faces, because God won't answer them.

**Leviticus 20:27** - A man also or woman that hath a familiar spirit, or that is a wizard, shall surely be put to death: they shall stone them with stones: their blood [shall be] upon them.

**Deuteronomy 18:10 -** There shall not be found among you any one that maketh his son or his daughter to pass through the fire, or that useth divination, or an observer of times, or an enchanter, or a witch,

## PRAYER

*Father in the Name of Jesus Christ, I thank You for giving me authority over the devil and evil spirits.*

*I thank You that whatever I bind here on earth is bound in heaven and whatever I loose is loosed.*

*This day and forever, O LORD, I declare my authority over the devil, his agents, and demons. I confess that according to Your WORD, LORD, I have authority over demons and evil spirits. They are subject to my commands and decrees henceforth.*

*I now banish all evil messengers and monitoring spirits from hell assigned against my life and family.*

*I decree paralysis for every demonic messenger, evil watchers, fowlers, spiritual hunters, and every agent of darkness working to cause me shame and loss.*

*I command them to become permanently disabled from this day forward, in Jesus name.*

---

*O LORD, it is written that they shall gather together, but their gathering is not of YOU. Whoever gathers against me shall scatter and fall (Isaiah 54:17).*

*I, therefore, command this day, let a furious east wind from heaven confuse, scatter and paralyze every evil gathering against my life and my family in the name of Jesus Christ.*

---

*I decree this day, let every satanic altar and court existing against my life and family, raising accusations and counter-accusations against me and my destiny, be destroyed by fire.*

*Every demonic lawyer and judge giving judgments against my life, family and destiny, in the spirit, wherever you are, I command you all to die by fire in the name of Jesus Christ.*

*I nullify every evil judgment and decision that has been made and is being carried out against my life and family. I command all those carrying out such judgments against my family and me to become frustrated, in Jesus name.*

---

*It is written that all power belongs to God, now and forever (1 Peter 5:11).*

*I, therefore, bring anyone, physical or spiritual, claiming power and authority over my life, I bring them to judgment with God's WORD.*

*They have not dared me; they have dared God instead. And as the devil was overthrown in heaven for daring God, I command them to be deposed from controlling* and working against my life and destiny, in Jesus name.

---

Let the imagination of every satanic monitor fail and tumble into the abyss.

Let every witchcraft mirrors and crystal balls, monitoring my star break and scatter, in the name of Jesus Christ.

---

All monitoring agents across the oceans, on contract against my destiny, receive blindness and paralysis.

You eye that monitors me and attempts to cut off my breakthroughs, receive total blindness and paralysis today.

You powers that are investigating my future, fail by fire, in the name of Jesus Christ

---

Why do the nations rage and the people plot a vain thing? The kings of the earth set themselves, and the *rulers take counsel together, against the Lord and His Anointed, saying, "Let us break their bonds in pieces and cast away Their cords from us."*

*He who sits in the heavens shall laugh; the Lord shall hold them in derision. Then He shall speak to them in His wrath and distress them in His deep displeasure* **(PSALM 2:1-5)**.

---

*₁Plead my cause, O Lord, with those who strive with me; fight against those who fight against me.*

*₂Take hold of shield and buckler, and stand up for my help.*

*₃Also draw out the spear, and stop those who pursue me. Say to my soul, "I am your salvation."*

*₄Let those be put to shame and brought to dishonor who seek after my life; let those be turned back and brought to confusion who plot my hurt.*

*₅Let them be like chaff before the wind, and let the angel of the Lord chase them.*

₆*Let their way be dark and slippery, and let the angel of the Lord pursue them.*

₇*For without cause they have hidden their net for me in a pit, which they have dug without cause for my life.*

₈*Let destruction come upon him unexpectedly, and let his net that he has hidden catch himself; into that very destruction let him fall.*

*In Jesus name. (PSALM 35:1-8)*

---

*O Lord, I will live to eat the fruit of my labor.*

*Any man or woman, witch or wizard, who has vowed that I will not see good in life, let fire from heaven visit them and destroy their curses in Jesus name.*

---

*I command all spiritual arrows intended or released against me, my life, family, and marriage to go back to the sender.*

*Every grave dug against my family and me, O LORD, I close them in the mighty name of Jesus Christ.*

*May every curse, spell, charm, invoked against my life, may all the plans of the wicked agents of darkness perish today, in Jesus name.*

---

*Whatever I have eaten in the dream, causing problems in my body and destiny, I command them to be uprooted in Jesus name.*

---

*Whatever belongs to my life spiritually, physically and financially, that has been damaged by the curse and works of witchcraft, monitoring demons, and wicked individuals... be restored back a hundredfold.*

*I decree a total restoration of all lost opportunities and blessings for my life, family, and destiny, in Jesus name.*

---

*From this day, O LORD, I receive divine fire for supernatural speed in life.*

*I command distinguishing breakthrough to fall upon me.*

*When I lie down to sleep, I shall sleep in peace.*

*I shall only have dreams of the LORD and visions from heaven.*

*I shall no longer be oppressed in any way in my dreams..*

*I will manifest excellence in all that I do.*

*Favor is following me everywhere I go from today.*

*I receive supernatural breakthrough ideas, in Jesus name.*

THANK YOU, LORD, FOR ANSWERED PRAYERS.

## Prayer 10: Minister To Yourself

The following prayers are intended to guide you to minister to yourself using the anointing oil and the Holy Communion. Please read the following scriptures out loud...

**Mathew 15:13:** *But he answered and said, "Every plant, which my heavenly Father hath not planted, shall be rooted up."*

**Exodus 23:25-26:** *Worship the Lord your God, and his blessing will be on your food and water. I will take away sickness from among you, and none will miscarry or be barren in your land. I will give you a full lifespan.*

**James 5:13-15:** *Is anyone of you suffering? He should pray. Is anyone cheerful? He should sing praises. Is anyone of you sick? He should call the elders of the church to pray over him and anoint him with oil in the name of the Lord.*

*And the prayer offered in faith will restore the one who is sick. The Lord will raise him up. If he has sinned, he will be forgiven....*

## PRAY

**(Take a portion of the oil in your hand and lay your hand upon your head)**

*O LORD, according to Your word, every tree you have not planted shall be rooted out and every chaff burned with fire.*

*I, therefore, ask that the Fire of the Holy Spirit will trace every satanic seed and plantation in my life and let them be destroyed.*

*Every seed of laziness, disappointment, spiritual deafness, bareness, sin, confusion, frustration, and setback, be destroyed today by fire in the name of Jesus Christ.*

---

*LORD, it is written that as I serve You, You will take sickness and disease away from my family and me and none shall be barren.*

*It is also written in 3 John 1: 2 that You want us to prosper and be in good health. And in Psalm 107: 20,* that You sent Your Word, and Your Word heals us from every disease.

I pray this moment, LORD, take away every sickness and disease from me, in Jesus name.

---

O LORD, I ask that Your Spirit will energize and help me to always listen to Your voice and harken to your instruction.

Help me always to study Your Word and follow your direction for my life. And by this, I confess that I will live the days of my life in health and prosperity, in Jesus name.

---

It is written in Isaiah 53:4-5 and 2 Peter 2:24 that **"Christ took away my sorrows and carried my infirmities and diseases in his body at the cross. He was pierced for my sins and inabilities. The punishment and blow he suffered on the cross was for the peace. By his stripes, I am healed."**

*I, therefore, anoint myself according to the WORD of God; O LORD, let your healing power move all over my body right now in Jesus name.*

---

*Every spirit behind this disease and affliction, I curse you in the name of the lord, and I command you to leave my life and never return.*

*I command this sickness (name it) to wither out of my body this moment in Jesus mighty name.*

---

*It is written in Job 22:28, that I shall decree a thing and it shall be established, and light will shine on my ways. It is also written in the Mathew 18:18 that whatever I forbid here on earth will be prohibited in heaven and what I approve of will approved.*

*I decree an end to all forms of spiritual attacks in my life and family today.*

*You evil spirit fighting and oppressing my life, family, business, finances, dreams and spiritual life, I bind and cast you all into the abyss in Jesus name.*

*It is written that whoever the son sets free shall be free indeed. Jesus has set me free; I am free indeed.*

*My family is free; my body is free, my children are free, my business and my marriage and my career are set free.*

*My destiny is set free to shine from now onwards ........in the name of Jesus Christ.*

---

*Every evil spirit organized and projected to enforce bareness, miscarriage, shame, and delay in my life and family, I bind and cast you all into the abyss in Jesus name.*

According to Genesis 1:28, I have a covenant with fruitfulness. I am fruitful, in Jesus name.

---

*I shall walk in wisdom, knowledge and the fear of God. I shall not die before my time. I shall live and continue to declare the goodness of the lord. In Jesus name.*

*The wind of favor is blowing in every aspect of my life and family; I shall walk in financial prosperity from now onwards. Everyone and everything is working for my good, In Jesus name.*

---

## TAKE THE HOLY COMMUNION AND PRAY

*O Lord, my Father, King of Kings and LORD of lords. As I take this communion, I am joined to the Body and Blood of Jesus Christ. Whatever cannot afflict Christ has no place in my life.*

*It is written in Ephesians 2:6 that I am raised up with Christ and seated with Him in the heavenly places, far above all principalities and powers, above sickness and diseases.*

*LORD Jesus, by eating your flesh and drinking Your Blood, I have eternal life working in me henceforth. The life I live now is free from sorrows, sickness, and disease.*

*By this communion representing the Body and Blood of Jesus Christ, I decree that I belong only to the covenant sealed with the Blood of Jesus Christ, in Jesus name.*

---

*I decree according to Psalm 5:12 that I will be blessed and compassed roundabout with favor. The Lord has risen for me and favor me will begin to speak for me. All closed doors against my life are open from now onwards.*

*May the hearts of men and women work in my favor henceforth, in Jesus name.*

## Prayer 11: Thank God For Your Deliverance

**(Sing and dance before the Lord and the declare His praise from your mouth)**

*O Lord, It is written in Obadiah 1:17: But upon mount Zion shall be deliverance, and there shall be holiness, and the house of Jacob shall possess their possessions.*

*I have appeared on Your mount and prayed, so Lord, thank You for my deliverance. I am now possessing my possessions, in Jesus name.*

*Prosperity is mine.*

*Divine health is mine.*

*Peace and promotion is mine.*

*I am protected from evil.*

*In the name of Jesus Christ.*

*O Lord, You have saved me from the lion's mouth. You have delivered me from the wild ox. You have freed me from the devourer's cage. I shall stand and testify of your goodness before the congregation of your people.*

*You are the Lord God Almighty. Your praise and glory fills the earth. Your praise fills my life.*

*I thank You, Lord, with all my heart;*

*I sing praise to You before the gods. I face your holy Temple, bow down, and praise Your name because of your constant love and faithfulness, because you have shown that Your name and Your commands are supreme. You answered me when I called to you; with Your strength, you strengthened me.*

*O Lord, even though You are so high above, You care for the lowly, and the proud cannot hide from you.*

**You will do everything you have promised; Lord, Your love is eternal. You will complete the work that you have begun,n Jesus name.**

Amen.

# Chapter 6: How to Maintain Your Deliverance

*"When the unclean spirit has gone out of a person, it passes through waterless places seeking rest, but finds none. Then it says, 'I will return to my house from which I came.' And when it comes, it finds the house empty, swept, and put in order.*

*Then it goes and brings with it seven other spirits more evil than itself, and they enter and dwell there, and the last state of that person is worse than the first. So also will it be with this evil generation."* – **Matt. 12:43-45**

Jesus is saying here that there is a probability that one gets healed or delivered from something, and the problem comes back, and the situation even becomes worse. Not because the person wasn't healed in the first instance, but because the person did not care to maintain his healing.

But it doesn't have to be so.

Beyond getting delivered, God wants us to live free from all oppressions; He wants us to be strong and sound. Here are ways to maintain your healing:

## 1. Practice Advance Forgiveness

Advance forgiveness is forgiving an offense even before it is committed against you. You decide not to harbor hurts and bitterness no matter what. This is because as long as we're on earth, offenses will always come. As we're trying to let one issue go, something happens, and if we're not careful, we'll find ourselves, back and forth, always struggling with hurts from time to time.

Sit down today and tell yourself, *"LORD, help me to forgive offenses and issues even before they happen, in Jesus name."*

Life is too precious to live one moment is someone else's cage.

## 2. Allow No Vacuum in Your Mind.

You've heard that "Nature abhors a vacuum." That's right.

If you allow a vacuum in your mind, something will fill it. If you don't fill your mind with positive things, negative things will automatically load it. There can be no vacuum.

The Bible says: *"Keep this Book of the Law always on your lips; meditate on it day and night, so that you may be careful to do everything written in it. Then you will be prosperous and successful.* - **Joshua 1:8"**

Read the Bible daily, hear faith-filled tapes, and fill your mind with news and stuff that edifies you.

## 3. Get Busy for God

A free life is God's covenant to those who serve Him. You don't have to be a pastor to serve God. There are many service related things you can do to keep yourself connected to God's covenant. Join in sharing tracts, pray genuinely for others, become a volunteer in some community service, go pray for the sick from time to time, reach out to the poor, and so on. Just get busy for the LORD, and no enemy will have grounds over your life

## 4. Learn to Exercise Your Authority and Faith

It is possible that you experience some form challenges from time to time. Now, this doesn't mean you're no longer free from what you prayed against or that God did not deliver you as you prayed earlier. When you encounter these temporary situations, continually declare the Word of God over your health, even if you take medicines.

*Now faith is the assurance (title deed, confirmation) of things hoped for (divinely guaranteed), and the evidence of things not seen [the conviction of their reality—faith comprehends as fact what cannot be experienced by the physical senses]. 2 For by this [kind of] faith the [a]men of old gained [divine] approval -* **Hebrews 11:1(AMP).**

## 6. Use Your Words Right

**Proverbs 18:21** - Death and life are in the power of the tongue: and they that love it shall eat the fruit thereof.
**1 Peter 3:10** - For he that will love life, and see good days, let him refrain his tongue from evil, and his lips that they speak no guile
**Ephesians 4:29** - Let no corrupt communication proceed out of your mouth, but that which is suitable to the use of edifying, that it may minister grace unto the hearers.

# GOD BLESS YOU

# Get in Touch

We love testimonies. We love to hear what God is doing around the world as people draw close to Him in prayer. Please share your story with us.

Also, please consider giving this book a review on Amazon, and checking out our other titles at: www.amazon.com/author/danielokpara .

I also request that you check out our website at www.BetterLifeWorld.org, and consider joining our newsletter, which we send out once in a while with great tips, testimonies, and revelations from God's Word for victorious living.

Feel free to drop us your prayer request. We will join faith with you, and God's power will be released in your life and the issue in question

## About the Author

Daniel Chika Okpara is an influential voice in contemporary Christian ministry, with a vision to:

1. Bring others to Christ through the preaching of the Gospel with the demonstration of power of the Holy Spirit.

2. Establish believers in the Word through real-life teachings, and

3. Empower believers to become Ambassadors of the Kingdom who are bringing others to Christ and Occupying till the Coming of Christ.

He is the founder and CEO of Better Life World Outreach Ministries, a non-denominational ministry committed to global evangelism, and empowering of God's people with insights for victorious living.

He is also the founder of www.BreakthroughPrayers.org , an online portal leading people all over the world to encounter God and change their lives through prayer.

He is the author of over 50 life-transforming books on prayer, faith, entrepreneurship, relationship, and victorious living

WEBSITE: www.betterlifeworld.org

BOOKS: www.amazon.com/author/danielokpara

# Other Books By the Same Author

1. Prayer Retreat: 21 Days Devotional With Over 500 Prayers & Declarations to Destroy Stubborn Demonic Problems.

2. HEALING PRAYERS & CONFESSIONS

3. 200 Violent Prayers for Deliverance, Healing, and Financial Breakthrough.

4. Hearing God's Voice in Painful Moments

5. Healing Prayers: Prophetic Prayers that Brings Healing

6. Healing WORDS: Daily Confessions & Declarations to Activate Your Healing.

7. Prayers That Break Curses and Spells and Release Favors and Breakthroughs.

8. 120 Powerful Night Prayers That Will Change Your Life Forever.

9. How to Pray for Your Children Everyday

10. How to Pray for Your Family

11. Daily Prayer Guide

12. Make Him Respect You: 31 Very Important Relationship Advice for Women to Make their Men Respect them.

13. How to Cast Out Demons from Your Home, Office & Property

14. Praying Through the Book of Psalms

15. The Students' Prayer Book

16. How to Pray and Receive Financial Miracle

17. Powerful Prayers to Destroy Witchcraft Attacks.

18. Deliverance from Marine Spirits

19. Deliverance From Python Spirit

20. Anger Management God's Way

21. How God Speaks to You

22. Deliverance of the Mind

23. 20 Commonly Asked Questions About Demons

24. Praying the Promises of God

25. When God Is Silent! What to Do When Prayer Seems Unanswered or Delayed

26. I SHALL NOT DIE: Prayers to Overcome the Spirit and Fear of Death.

27. Praise Warfare

28. Prayers to Find a Godly Spouse

# NOTES

Made in the USA
Columbia, SC
19 August 2024